Englishcraft

F. F. Mann

of the English Department
Colbayns High School, Clacton-on-Sea

& A. J. Smith

Deputy Headmaster,
The Harwich School, Harwich

Bell & Hyman

Published in 1986 by
BELL & HYMAN LIMITED
Denmark House
37–39 Queen Elizabeth Street
London SE1 2QB

© F. F. Mann and A. J. Smith 1980
First published in 1980 by University Tutorial Press
Reprinted 1983 (with minor corrections)
Reprinted by Bell & Hyman Limited 1986

All rights reserved. No part of this publication may be reproduced, stored in a retrieval system, or transmitted in any form or by any means, electronic, mechanical, photo-copying, recording or otherwise without the prior permission of Bell & Hyman Limited.

British Library Cataloguing in Publication Data

Mann, F. F.
   Englishcraft.
   1
   1. English language—Examinations, questions, etc.
   2. English language—Composition and exercises
   I. Title   II. Smith, A. J. (Anthony John)
   428.2   PE1112

ISBN 0-7135-2639-4

Other books by F. Mann and A. Smith, published by Bell & Hyman, include:
Englishcraft 2
Englishcraft 3
English in Practice Book 1
English in Practice Book 2

Also by A. Smith:
Clear Punctuation

Printed and bound in Great Britain by
William Clowes Limited, Beccles and London

Contents

Starting point   1

1 Writing in detail

Thinking about your audience	2
'Shadow in the gallery' from *The Giant under the Snow* by John Gordon	2
Sentences and phrases	5
Writing a description of a place	7
The great gales rage in the trees, a poem by George Barker	8
Writing your own poem	9
Avoiding the excessive use of 'and'	10
Imagining in detail	10
'The tunnel' from *Pirate's Island* by John Rowe Townsend	11
Writing a story	13
Vocabulary: words suggesting sounds	13
Pleasant sounds, a poem by John Clare	15
Writing your own poem	15
Further reading	16

2 Use your senses

'Under the table' from *The Peppermint Pig* by Nina Bawden	17
A good beginning	19
Hide and seek, a poem by Vernon Scannell	21
Writing your own poem	22
Statements, questions and commands	23
'Cold cloth and frozen buttons' from *Sand* by William Mayne	24
Openings	25
Nouns	27
Letter-writing	28
Further reading	31

3 Writing about animals

'Bubble and Squeak' from *The Battle of Bubble and Squeak* by Philippa Pearce	33
Writing instructions	35
Take one home for the kiddies, a poem by Philip Larkin	36
Writing your own poem	37
Nouns	37
Letter-writing	37
'Pussy' from *Widdershins Crescent* by John Rowe Townsend	38
The end	40
Commas	41
Writing your own poem	43
Using a dictionary	44
Vocabulary: nouns formed from people's names	45
Further reading	45

4 Christmas

'The carol-singers' from *The Wind in the Willows* by Kenneth Grahame	47
Writing a story	50
Commas	50
Wassailers	51
Mummers' play	52
Carols	56
Writing your own poem	58
Writing a story	58
Pronouns	60
Further reading	61

5 Waiting for the bell

Starting school	62
First day at school, a poem by Roger McGough	63
Writing an account	64
'Three pieces of soap' from *Grandad with Snails*, by Michael Baldwin	65
Adjectives	66
Writing your own poem	69

'The new boy' from *The Dragon in the Garden* by Reginald Maddock	69
Choosing powerful adjectives	71
Writing a description	72
Revision of punctuation	72
Vocabulary: nouns from place-names; loan words	73
Further reading	74

6 Writing about the past

'The survivor' from *Dawn Wind* by Rosemary Sutcliff	75
Writing a story	77
Verbs	78
Treasure!	81
The hoard, a poem by J R R Tolkien	81
Writing your own poem	84
Apostrophes	84
'Fur and fang' from *Mist over Athelney* by Geoffrey Trease	85
Riddles	87
Writing your own poem	88
'Fire!' from *Wordhoard* by Jill Paton Walsh and Kevin Crossley-Holland	88
Writing a story	90
Vocabulary	92
Further reading	92

7 The moon and back

Writing about the future	94
Space travellers, a poem by James Nimmo	94
Writing your own poem	95
Moon landing	96
'Lunar journey' from *The Lotus Caves* by John Christopher	97
Verbs	98
Writing a story	100
Apostrophes	101
Vocabulary: suffixes to form verbs	102
Off course, a poem by Edwin Morgan	103
Writing your own poem	103

'The fun they had' a short story from *The Earth is Room Enough* by Isaac Asimov	104
Writing an account	107
Letter-writing	107
Further reading	108

8 Conversations

'I want to report a murder' from *Run for your Life* by David Line	109
Play-writing	111
Direct speech	112
Writing a conversation	114
'The woodwork lesson' from *Mike and Me* by David Line	115
Vocabulary: prefixes	116
Writing a story	117
Adverbs	117
A landscape tale and *When the ceiling cries*, poems by Russell Edson	118
Writing your own poem	120
Further reading	120

9 The supernatural

'The haunting' from *The Ghost of Thomas Kempe* by Penelope Lively	121
Play-writing	123
Subject and predicate	123
By St Thomas Water, a poem by Charles Causley	125
Similes	128
Writing your own poem	129
Direct speech	129
Writing a conversation	130
'Long-ago voices' from *The Ghosts* by Antonia Barber	130
Vocabulary: suffixes to form adjectives	131
Letter-writing	133
Writing a story	133
Further reading	133

10 Summer and swallows

Looking back	135
'Like a cork' from *The Battle of Wednesday Week* by Barbara Willard	135
Writing a description	137
Subject and predicate	138
The arrival, a poem by John Walsh	140
Holiday towns	141
Writing an article	142
Writing your own poem	142
'The boat' from *Goldengrove* by Jill Paton Walsh	142
Writing a story	145
Revision of punctuation	145
Work and play, a poem by Ted Hughes	146
Writing your own poem	148
Vocabulary	148
Further reading	148

Acknowledgements

Drawings are by KEITH HOWARD.

The authors and publishers are grateful to the following for permission to use copyright material:
John Gordon for the extract from *The Giant under the Snow* (Hutchinson Publishing Group Ltd);
George Barker for 'The great gales rage in the trees' reprinted by permission of Faber & Faber Ltd from *Poems of Places and People* by George Barker;
John Rowe Townsend for the extract from *Pirate's Island* by permission of Oxford University Press;
Nina Bawden for the extract from *The Peppermint Pig* (Victor Gollancz Ltd);
Vernon Scannell for 'Hide and seek' from *Selected Poems* (Allison & Busby Ltd);
William Mayne for the extract from *Sand* (Hamish Hamilton Ltd);
Philippa Pearce for the extract from *The Battle of Bubble and Squeak* (Andre Deutsch Ltd);
Philip Larkin for 'Take one home for the kiddies' reprinted by permission of Faber & Faber Ltd from *The Whitsun Weddings* by Philip Larkin;
John Rowe Townsend for the extract from *Widdershins Crescent* (Hutchinson Publishing Group Ltd);
Kenneth Grahame for the extract from *The Wind in the Willows*, text copyright University Chest, Oxford;
A L Lloyd for the wassail song from *Folk Song in England* (Lawrence & Wishart Ltd);
the British Library for the Mummers' play from Romsey, Hampshire, from John Latham *Collection for a history of Romsey, Hampshire.* Reproduced by permission of the Trustees of the British Museum. Additional MS 26778, ff. 4–5v (Romsey Mummers' play);
Roger McGough for 'First day at school' from *In the Glassroom* (Jonathan Cape Ltd);

Michael Baldwin for the extract from *Grandad with Snails* (Routledge & Kegan Paul Ltd);
Reginald Maddock for the extract from *The Dragon in the Garden* by permission of Macmillan, London and Basingstoke;
Rosemary Sutcliff for the extract from *Dawn Wind* by permission of Oxford University Press;
J R R Tolkien for 'The hoard' from *The Adventures of Tom Bombadil* (George Allen & Unwin (Publishers) Ltd);
Geoffrey Trease for the extract from *Mist over Athelney* by permission of Macmillan, London and Basingstoke;
Kevin Crossley-Holland for two riddles from *The Battle of Maldon and other Old English Poems* (Macmillan) © Kevin Crossley-Holland and Bruce Mitchell 1965;
Jill Paton Walsh for the extract from 'Thurkell the Tall' from *Wordhoard* by permission of Macmillan, London and Basingstoke;
Henry Treece for the extract from *The Horned Helmet* (Hodder & Stoughton Ltd);
John Christopher for the extracts from *The Lotus Caves* (Hamish Hamilton Ltd);
Edwin Morgan for 'Off Course' from *From Glasgow to Saturn* (Carcanet Press Ltd);
Isaac Asimov for 'The fun they had' from *The Earth is Room Enough* (Abelard-Schuman Ltd);
David Line for the extracts from *Run for your Life* and *Mike and Me* (Jonathan Cape Ltd);
Penelope Lively for the extract from *The Ghost of Thomas Kempe* (William Heinemann Ltd);
Charles Causley for 'By St Thomas Water' from *Collected Poems* (Macmillan);
Antonia Barber for the extract from *The Ghosts* (Jonathan Cape Ltd);
Barbara Willard for the extract from *The Battle of Wednesday Week* (Kestrel Books);
Mrs A M Walsh for 'The arrival' from *The Truants* by John Walsh;
Jill Paton Walsh for the extract from *Goldengrove* by permission of Macmillan, London and Basingstoke;
Ted Hughes for 'Work and play' by permission of Faber & Faber Ltd from *Season Songs* by Ted Hughes.

The publishers would also like to acknowledge brief quotations from the following:
Nina Bawden *Squib, The Runaway Summer, The White Horse Gang, On the Run, A Handful of Thieves* (Victor Gollancz Ltd);
William Mayne *The Incline, Thumstick, The Jersey Shore*, (Hamish Hamilton Ltd);
Susan Cooper *Over Sea, Under Stone, The Dark is Rising*, (Chatto & Windus Ltd);
Barbara Willard *Harrow and Harvest* (Kestrel Books);
Ray Bradbury *A Sound of Thunder, Hail and Farewell*;
H E Bates *Time to Kill*;
Margaret Williams *Wordhoard*.

In spite of every effort the publishers have been unable to trace the copyright holders of 'When the ceiling cries' and 'A landscape tale' by Russell Edson and 'Space travellers' by James Nimmo.

Thanks are due to the following for the use of photographs:

pps 14, 42, 137 J Allan Cash Ltd; pps 22, 132 Nick Thompson; p 36 J B Briggs; pps 43, 68 Will Green; p 54 (Brian Shuel photographer) Vaughan Williams Memorial Library; pps 80, 84, 93 reproduced by Courtesy of the Trustees of the British Museum; p 83 The Ashmolean Museum; p 95 NASA.

The answers to the riddles on page 88 are
1   A swan
2   Fire.

Starting point

English is the most important subject that you study. This book is to help you to write well. Often it is felt that some people are born to write well and that everybody else will always lack this ability. Most people can, however, with hard work, clear guidance and practice become skilful writers.

Writing is a craft. It can be mastered by you if you are determined to succeed in it. If you want to write well you need to look at work of very skilful writers and think about the lessons you can learn from them. Reading will provide you with ideas and widen your vocabulary. You also need advice on techniques which will help your work. Above all, you need to practise carefully, trying your best in every piece of writing that you do. When you have finished it, read it carefully. After your teacher has marked it and commented on it, think how it could have been improved, and try to make the improvement when you next write.

We hope you will find the advice in this book useful and that the passages and poems will make you want to read more works by these writers.

1 Writing in detail

Thinking about your audience

When an actor is on a stage, he knows that he has an audience. He tries to communicate with them, to show them how he sees the character that he has been chosen to play, and to keep their interest. He knows whether or not he has succeeded by the way that the audience feel about his performance.

An author who writes a novel is also trying to communicate with people and to interest them. He usually has a clear idea of the people he hopes will read his work. The author also judges his success by the reactions of his readers, his audience.

When you write a story, an essay, a letter or a poem, and even when you are carrying out an exercise, you are writing *for* someone. A letter is usually sent to a single person. If you know the person, it is not difficult to see what will interest him or her. Other work may be written for your teacher or your friends. Sometimes your writing may have a wider audience, if it is to be displayed in the classroom, or printed in the school magazine.

Before you start to write anything, always consider for whom you are writing, and what your readers want.

Sometimes you may write only for yourself, and even if your work is going to be read by others, *you* should always be the most demanding reader.

Shadow in the gallery

If you want to make your readers believe in what you have written you must write in detail. In the following passage John Gordon presents many details of the museum, which show that he had a very clear picture of it in his mind. These details were ones that he had noticed and remembered. They make the museum real for us, and help us to believe what happens there.

Jonk Winters had found an ancient buckle. With two friends, Arf and Bill, she had taken it to the local museum which owned the belt to which the buckle belonged. They were in the museum at closing time, when the lights were being put out. The children were about to go out into the darkness of a December evening, but someone else wanted the belt and its buckle.

. . . The shadow came up slowly, broadened until it filled the bottom pane, and then the figure came into view. A massive head on broad sloping shoulders pressed silently towards them. They could see no face, but they knew that in the dark side of the head deep gashes of eyes were levelled in their direction.

'It's him!' Jonk was shrinking back.

Bill took control. 'The gallery,' he said. 'Quick!'

They retreated into the blackness, nudged by the corners of the showcases which seemed always to bar their way. Bill held Jonk's sleeve. His foot kicked the bottom stair.

'Arf!'

Arf had become separated from them.

'Arf!'

'Yes.' He had missed the foot of the stairs and was wandering somewhere to their left.

'Here!' said Bill.

Arf was fumbling towards them as they heard the door handle begin to turn.

'Hurry, hurry!' said Jonk. She began to back up the stairs as she felt over the banisters for Arf. His coat brushed her hand as the front door bell kicked and jangled. They saw both halves of the door swing inwards. A dog's feet rattled on the lino.

With a hideous slowness they climbed backwards as though a black tide was rising at their feet. They could hear the dog running to and fro in the foyer. The front door was out of sight but enough light came through from outside to show them the arched doorway into the hall. A shadow fell across it. They reached the top of the stairs and crouched behind the railings.

'Keep down, right down.' Bill's voice was barely audible.

They lay flat, their faces to the bars, listening to the paws. The dog was in the hall below. There was no sound from the man. None. But the well of the hall seemed full of him. It was a black, aching hole in which he was gliding. He may be anywhere. Perhaps climbing the stairs. His foot might at any second crush them. They did not breathe.

The dog stopped. There was complete silence and then, like a cruel wind creaking the door of an abandoned house, came a laugh. It gibbered in the hall, finding its way through cracks in the air to rake their hair with bony fingers and tug at their scalps. They felt themselves being drawn out of hiding by it and they clung to the bars while it swept over them.

JOHN GORDON *The Giant under the Snow*

Talking about the passage

1 What do we learn about the museum?
2 What are we told about the mysterious figure who was with the dog?
3 How does the writer make us imagine the sounds as the children listened in the darkness?
4 Why were the children unable to escape?

Writing about the passage

Write answers to the following questions. To help you, the beginning of each answer has been given.

1 Describe the shape of the figure that entered the museum.
   The figure that entered the museum had ...

2   Why did the children find it difficult to reach the gallery?
    The children found it difficult to reach the gallery because . . .
3   How did the children try to prevent the man from finding them?
    The children tried to prevent the man from finding them by . . .
4   What did the laugh seem to do to the children?
    The laugh seemed to . . .
5   How would you have felt if you had been one of the children there?
    If I had been one of the children there, I would have felt . . .
6   If you had been there, what would you have done?
    If I had been there, I would have . . .

Sentences and phrases

You should always write in sentences. A *sentence* is a group of words which may stand by itself and make complete sense. The following groups of words are all sentences:

The sun is shining. (a statement)
Is it too hot in here? (a question)
Open the window. (a command)

A *statement* is a sentence which tells us what someone or something is or does. It always begins with a capital letter and ends with a full stop:
They did not breathe.
The dog stopped.

Connected groups of words which cannot stand by themselves are called *phrases*.

during the afternoon
   This group of words cannot stand by itself and make complete sense. It tells us a time, but it does not tell us what happened at that time. The group of words is therefore a phrase.
as quickly as possible
   This group of words is also a phrase. It tells us how something was done, but it does not tell us what was done.
at the corner of the street
   This group of words tells us where something was done, but it does not tell us what was done. It is therefore another phrase.

The following groups of words are all sentences, as they can stand by themselves and make complete sense:

During the afternoon I went to the cinema.
He ran away as quickly as possible.
At the corner of the street I met my friends.

Exercise 1

Write out the groups of words below, and say whether each is a sentence or a phrase. Begin each sentence with a capital letter, and end it with a full stop.

1   i went to stay with my aunt
2   she lives in a small cottage
3   on the first day of my holiday
4   her garden was neat and full of flowers
5   my favourite flower
6   as carefully as she could
7   i helped to weed the garden
8   the roses were beginning to wilt
9   on the biggest of the apple trees
10 the pears would soon be ripe

Exercise 2

Write a complete sentence in answer to each of the following questions.

1   What is your name?
2   Where do you live?
3   How old are you?
4   Which school do you attend?
5   How far from the school do you live?
6   How do you travel to school?
7   What is the name of your form-teacher?
8   What is the name of your English teacher?
9   How do you like to spend your spare time?
10 What kind of books do you most like to read?

Exercise 3

The following description of a classroom consists of a series of statements. Rewrite the passage correctly. Each statement should begin with a capital letter and end with a full stop.

the classroom is large its walls are painted blue along one side of the room there are four wide windows from these windows you can see the playground the door is on the other side of the room the blackboard takes up most of a third wall the desks of the pupils are arranged in four rows the desk at which the teacher sits is in front of the blackboard a cupboard stands beside his desk there are pictures on the pinboard at the back of the room

Exercise 4

Write an exact description, in a series of statements, of the classroom in which you have your English lessons. Include as much detail as possible.

Writing a description of a place

John Gordon gives a clear picture in words of what you would have seen inside the museum. In order to test your powers of observation write a description of the street or area where you live. Try to include as many details as possible, so that the reader gains an idea of why your street is special – no two streets are exactly alike. Have a definite time of year in mind for your description, as every place changes according to the season.

Before you begin to write, make notes about the street. The following questions might help you:

1 In what area is the street?
2 What are the houses like? How many floors do they have? Are they well-decorated on the whole?
3 What special features are seen in particular houses?
4 What are the gardens like?
5 How much traffic uses the street? Do cars park there?

6   What kinds of people are to be seen in the street? Do children play there?

Make your notes and then prepare a rough copy of your description. Read it through carefully. Does it give your reader a good idea of what your street is like? Improve it, and then write out a final copy.

The passage from *The Giant under the Snow* reminds us that sounds should be imagined in detail. Noting and remembering sounds are very important to the writer. You can see this in the following poem.

The great gales rage in the trees

The great gales rage in the trees outside the window.
   The moon races
over mottled water meadows and in shadows
   and moonlight the surfaces
   of the nightmare stream glint
and shiver in the wind as winter
   shrieks in the chimney stack
and not even the far obedient star
   believes it can ever bring
   the summer back.
The dog whimpers. A door slams. The shutters
   clap and a sleeping child
   stirs with a haunted sigh
   as the storm mutters
and groans around this dreaming and lonely
   house. From tossing trees
   the torn boughs
hang swaying dislocated, and uneasily
   the wood fire gutters
   as hisses and spits
   of rain sputter and drip
   into tiny blazes. I watch
   the year turning
   and burning to ash
   once more, once more
and hear the breathtaking grave-haunting wolf
   of death at the door.

GEORGE BARKER

Talking about the poem

1. At what time of year is the poem set?
2. Why does the moon seem to race?
3. How does the moonlight affect the landscape that can be seen from the window?
4. Which sounds can be heard from inside and outside the house?
5. What effects do the gales have upon the trees?
6. How does the rain affect the fire?
7. Which words in the poem have been chosen by George Barker because they suggest sounds?

Writing your own poem

Most of you will have written poems before. The obvious difference between poems and stories is in the way they are set out on the page, but the main difference between them is in the way that they 'move'. Poems have a pattern in their movement and in their sounds. You can see this in the lines at the end of *The great gales rage in the trees*.

>   ... I watch
>   the year turning
>   and burning to ash
>   once more, once more
> and hear the breathtaking grave-haunting wolf
>   of death at the door.

Here the poet has used a rhyme ('more' rhymes with 'door') but poetry does not have to rhyme. If you try to use rhyme, you may find that it takes over, till you become more concerned with finding rhyming words than you are with what you are saying. In a poem, as in any other kind of writing, you have something to tell the reader, and you must tell it as clearly and effectively as possible. As what you are saying is the most important thing, do not use rhyme if it causes too many problems for you.

Imagine that you are lying awake at night, unable to sleep. What time of year is it? What is the weather like? Think of what you might see inside the darkened room. Do those shapes remind you of something? What might you see through the curtains? Think of the sounds that you would hear from inside the house, and also from outside. What might the sounds suggest to you? Note down your thoughts on each of these matters.

When you have completed your notes, write a poem called 'Lying awake'. Remember, when you have written the first draft read it through, improve it and then copy it out neatly.

And

A common fault is to make writing boring by using the word 'and' too frequently. This causes a writer to use long sentences where shorter ones would be better. The fault may be seen in the passage below.

I climbed the ladder very carefully and I opened the trapdoor that led to the loft. After opening the trapdoor I clambered in, switching on the light, and I saw cobwebs hanging from the rafters, which were covered in dust. There was a water tank beside the trapdoor and there was also a cardboard box in a corner, that might contain the papers I was seeking. Stooping, I made my way across the loft to the box and when I reached the box I opened it and I found that it was full of old clothes. Although there was a cold draught, I did not know from where it was coming, and I could hear a rustling sound, but I did not know its cause. The rustling grew louder and the light suddenly went out, and I was left in the darkness, listening.

This passage may be improved by the removal of the word 'and', and the shortening of the sentences. For example, the last sentence will become three shorter sentences, which suggest far more strongly the fear which the person felt:
The rustling grew louder. The light suddenly went out. I was left in the darkness, listening.

Rewrite the whole passage removing the word 'and' and thus shortening the sentences, as in the example.

Imagining in detail

Often it is possible to set stories in places that you know. In these cases it is not difficult to tell your reader details which will make him or her feel that the place is real.

Sometimes, however, you will want to write about places which you have never seen. Then you must imagine the details. You have to invent sights, sounds and feelings that will make the place, and the events that happen there, come alive for your reader.

The writer of the next passage may never have waded through a river which flows through a dark tunnel but he imagines the experience in detail. This makes the reader feel that while he is reading the passage he is up to his knees in water and surrounded by darkness.

The tunnel

Two children, Sheila and Gordon, are in danger. They try to escape through a tunnel down which a shallow river flows. They are carrying a chest. It is night.

Where the roof of the tunnel was highest they could just stand upright, but that meant putting both feet in the water. Gordon, long past caring about wet feet, decided to try it. But the bed of the tunnel was slimy and the water-pressure stronger than he'd expected. It would be all too easy to lose your footing and be swept as if by a water-chute down into the canal. At the sides, the surface was still slippery but not so dangerously so, and you could feel for handholds along the wall as you went. But it meant bending almost double.

Gordon and Sheila slung the chest between them once more and set off along the tunnel, one at each side of the stream. There was a slight upward slope, but that was nothing much. It was not being able to straighten up that made their progress so painful. And after a few yards the darkness closed in. The patch of light behind them, where they'd entered the tunnel, soon dwindled. The far end was up in Claypits, where the river went underground, and that was a good mile away. The blackness was deeper than anything Gordon had ever known. He felt it like a woolly bandage over his eyes. He felt, too, the weight of all that earth above, laden with roads and railway lines and buildings, pressing down on him. He had a sudden terror of being buried alive.

He remembered the torch, still in his coat-pocket, and called to Sheila to stop. Taking a hand off the wall, he groped for the torch, switched it on, and transferred it to the hand that already held one end of the chest. It was awkward to manage, but he had to keep the other hand to guide himself. They trudged on for perhaps a quarter-mile, a little cheered by the light. And then Gordon slipped, went down full length, and dropped the torch in the water. In its rubber casing it floated easily. Before he could make a grab for it, it was out of reach. They watched it, still shining, as it was carried downstream away from them and out of sight. And all was total blackness again – blacker, it seemed, than ever.

JOHN ROWE TOWNSEND   *Pirate's Island*

Talking about the passage

1 Describe the inside of the tunnel.
2 Why was it difficult for the children to make their way along the tunnel?
3 Describe Gordon's feelings as he walked along in the darkness.
4 Why was the torch important to the children?

Writing about the passage

Answer the following questions in complete sentences. Part of the answer is given to help you.

1 Why would it have been dangerous for the children to walk where the roof of the tunnel was highest?
It would have been dangerous . . .
2 What difficulties did they find in walking along the sides of the tunnel?
In walking along the sides of the tunnel they found . . .
3 Why did Gordon feel as if he had a woolly bandage over his eyes?
Gordon felt . . .
4 What suddenly scared Gordon?
. . . scared Gordon.
5 Why did he have to hold the torch in the hand which already held one end of the chest?
He had to hold the torch . . .
6 When Gordon dropped the torch, why was he unable to recover it?
When Gordon . . .
7 What thoughts do you think went through the children's minds as the torch floated away?
As the torch floated away . . .
8 Why do many people fear darkness?
Many people fear darkness . . .

Writing a story

Write a story called 'A long walk home'. Imagine that you have to walk home alone on a dark night, when no street-lamps are alight. You need to have a definite idea of the time of year at which your account is set, and of the weather conditions. Just as John Rowe Townsend, in the passage from *Pirate's Island,* knows exactly what the tunnel looks like, so you should have a clear picture of the streets you are walking through. If you have such a picture, then details will come into your story which will make the scenes seem real to the reader.

Every story must have a beginning, a middle and an end. You are advised to begin when your walk is about to start, or when it is already taking place. End your story in such a way that the reader does not forget your feelings during the walk. You could end on a mysterious note, without arriving home, or you could end with a brief description of your relief at reaching safety. Try to include some exciting incidents, such as hearing strange sounds, or seeing shadows in the moonlight.

The more carefully you make notes before you start to write the better your story will be. Remember, after you have completed your rough draft read and revise it before copying out your final story.

Vocabulary

Many words are meant to suggest sounds. You can find some of these words in the passages you have already read, such as: shriek, whimper, slam, clap, sigh, mutter, groan, hiss, spit, sputter.

Often the simplest examples of such words represent sudden loud sounds, for example 'bang' and 'crack'. What other words suggest similar sounds?

For quiet or distant sounds we use words like 'rustle' and 'mutter'. Can you think of any others?

Give as many examples as possible of words representing each of the following:

1   animal noises
2   harsh grating sounds
3   pleasant musical sounds

Which other sounds can be captured in words?

Sometimes a word can be invented to suggest a sound for which no word exists. One writer used the word 'kinclunk' to describe the sound of a car passing over a loose manhole cover.

Create ten words of your own to represent sounds. Among the noises you might choose are the sounds of eating celery or spaghetti, of walking across mud, of a train moving quickly or slowly, of a flock of starlings or a single pigeon.

Pleasant sounds

The rustling of leaves under the feet in woods and under hedges;
The crumpling of cat-ice and snow down wood-rides, narrow lanes, and every street causeway;
Rustling through a wood or rather rushing, while the wind halloos in the oak-top like thunder;
The rustle of birds' wings startled from their nests or flying unseen into the bushes;
The whizzing of larger birds overhead in a wood, such as crows, puddocks, buzzards;
The trample of robins and woodlarks on the brown leaves, and the patter of squirrels on the green moss;
The fall of an acorn on the ground, the pattering of nuts on the hazel branches as they fall from ripeness;
The flirt of the groundlark's wing from the stubbles – how sweet such pictures on dewy mornings, when the dew flashes from its brown feathers!

JOHN CLARE

Talking about the poem

1 Which words are used to represent sounds in this poem?
2 How successfully has the poet chosen these words?
3 Could any of these words have been improved upon? If any could, suggest alternatives.

Writing your own poem

Write a poem called 'The sounds I hate'. Describe the sounds you hate most, and take care to choose words which suggest those sounds.

Exercise 5

At the beginning of this unit you were reminded that a sentence is a group of words which may stand by itself and make complete sense.
   Write a complete sentence about each of the following, describing the sounds which it makes.

1 the wind in the trees

2 the rusty hinges
3 the frightened child
4 the trumpets
5 the great waves
6 the angry crowd
7 the horse and cart
8 the drums and cymbals
9 the lonely puppy
10 the driving rain

Further reading

John Rowe Townsend, the writer of the second passage in this unit, has written many books. Among those that you might enjoy are the following:

Pirate's Island
Gordon Dobbs, the son of a pork-butcher, was fat. Known as 'Porky', he was bullied by other boys. Sheila, a waif, becomes his friend, and leads him into an adventure.

Gumble's Yard
Kevin and Sandra are the eldest of four abandoned children. They fight to keep the family together, even though this means a moonlight flit to a derelict warehouse on the canal bank. They, however, are not the only users of Gumble's Yard.

Widdershins Crescent
The family featured in *Gumble's Yard* moves to a new council estate, where the problems for Kevin and Sandra increase. Their greatest task is to try to stop the head of the household, their uncle Walter, from destroying it.

Hell's Edge
This novel is set in the Yorkshire town of Hallersage. A girl from the south clashes with her cousin, a tough local boy, until a problem for the town makes them join forces.

2 Use your senses

In unit 1 you were advised to imagine places and events in detail when writing about them. To do this successfully, you need to use all your senses.

We have five senses: sight, hearing, smell, touch and taste. When you are thinking of a place or an event, you should ask yourself certain questions:
If I were in that place or if that event were happening:

- What would I see?
- What would I hear?
- What would I smell?
- What would things feel like?
- What would I taste?

Perhaps not all of these questions will need answers. If you attempt to answer them, however, it will help you to create or remember the details that your work needs. The passages in this unit both show writers using their senses and making the reader use his or hers.

If a writer makes the reader use his or her senses from the very first words of a story or a passage, then he catches the reader's interest.

Under the table

. . . a dark day of thick, mustardy fog that had specks of grit in it she could taste on her tongue. Theo was not allowed out because of his delicate chest and by the time Poll got home from school she was already angry. She had been in a cold classroom all day, some of the time stuck in the corner with the Dunce's Cap on, made of green drawing paper and smelling of gum, while Mother and Theo had been cosy at home, sharing secrets. Poll loved Theo but she was jealous by nature and when she came coughing in from the fog, hands and feet cold as toads, and found him sitting on Mother's lap by the fire where she wanted to be, she wished he was dead. *She* was supposed to be the baby, wasn't she?

She was naughty at tea. Children were expected to behave well in those days and although Emily Greengrass was less strict in some ways than most mothers, she was firm about table manners. It was always, 'Sit up straight.' 'Don't talk with your mouth full.' 'Elbows off the table, I won't tell you again.'

That afternoon, Poll had to be told once too often. Her mother said, 'I've had enough, my girl. Under the table!'

Poll didn't mind. She had eaten as much as she wanted – she always ate a great deal, very fast, unlike Theo who chewed every mouthful so slowly that Mother's fresh scones, crisp and warm from the oven and dripping with butter, might have been dry lumps of old cardboard – and with a good tea inside her it was pleasant under the table. The starched white cloth hung down almost to the floor, making a good, private place where she could behave as she liked and no one to see. The linoleum was brown and patterned in criss-cross stripes of a lighter shade. Poll thought these looked like little gates, and pretending to be a baby again, tried to push them open with her fingers. She spat on the floor and blew on the spit, to see the colours change in the bubble. There

were spiders in the dusty underside of the table and she fetched one down and teased him by letting him run and then barring his way until she felt sorry and took off her shoe to give him a ride in it.

NINA BAWDEN   *The Peppermint Pig*

Talking about the passage

1 Why was Poll naughty at tea?
2 How did Poll feel when she had to go under the table?
3 What do we learn about her from the extract?
4 Can you remember any times when you felt as Poll did?

Writing about the passage

Answer the following questions in complete sentences.

1 Why was Theo not allowed out that day?
2 What had made Poll angry?
3 Describe Poll's feelings towards Theo.
4 Why did Emily Greengrass become annoyed with her daughter?
5 Why did Poll not mind when she was sent under the table?
6 How did she amuse herself there?
7 Poll felt that, under the table, she was in 'a private place'. Describe the private place you have or would like to have, and the activities you could carry out there.

A good beginning

A story is written to be read and enjoyed. A good beginning to a story is very important, as it will make your reader want to discover what happens next. There are many different ways in which you can start your stories in order to gain your reader's interest. You might open with an exciting situation, or begin by appealing to the senses, with a striking sound, sight, smell or taste.

    Writers know the value of an interesting start to their novels. Nina Bawden and William Mayne (who wrote the books from which the extracts in this unit are taken) have used various methods in beginning their stories. Below there is a selection of openings from their books. Read them carefully, and then discuss how these authors have tried to make the reader interested right at the beginning.

1   Mary was angry. She had been angry for ages: she couldn't remember when she had last felt nice. Sometimes she was angry for a good reason – when someone tried to make her do something she didn't want to do – but most of the time she was angry for no reason at all. She just woke in the morning feeling cross and miserable and as if she wanted to kick or break things.

NINA BAWDEN   *The Runaway Summer*

2   John's bedroom window faced north over Vendale. On fine mornings in the summer the sun shone through the window, on to the mirror, and then into his eyes, waking him up. The mirror had to be moved every few days or its reflection would miss his face. On wet days there was no sun to wake him, and nothing to wake for. The empty bright morning was the best part of his day, before the things that came in order from breakfast to supper.

WILLIAM MAYNE   *Thumstick*

3   There are two things to remember about adventures. They always happen when you are not expecting anything to happen and the beginning is usually quite unexciting and ordinary so that you seldom realise that something important has begun. Adventure always creeps up on you from behind.

NINA BAWDEN   *On the Run*

4   The journey lasted all night and all day. Even before the night had closed against the windows of the train Arthur had seen for long enough the ample horizons of America running along the edge of the sky. When the daylight deepened into blue twilight and then swooped into blackness he was glad to be able to stop looking from the window at a view that never became anything.

WILLIAM MAYNE   *The Jersey Shore*

5   His name was Squib. At least, that was what the little ones called him. 'There's Squib,' they shouted, racing across the shaved grass of the park to where he waited by the swings and the sandpit and the seesaw, a small, pale child, pale-skinned, pale-haired. Always alone – and lonely looking, too, which is not quite the same thing.

NINA BAWDEN   *Squib*

After you have read all the extracts, pick the one that you like best. Take this extract as the opening of a story of your own.

Remember the advice given to you in the last unit about imagining places and events in great detail.

Hide and seek

Yoo-hoo! I'm ready! Come and find me!
The sacks in the toolshed smell like the seaside.
You make yourself little in the salty dark,
Close your eyes tight and hope your feet aren't showing.
Better not risk another call, they might be close.
Don't sneeze whatever happens. The floor is cold.
They're probably searching the bushes near the swing.
What's that? That sounds like them. They're coming in!
Don't breathe or move. Still. Someone knocks a can.
Feet mutter. Somebody comes very close.
A scuffle of words, a laugh, and then they're gone.
They might be back. Careful in case they come.
They'll try the greenhouse, then in here again.
They're taking a long time, but they'll come back.
Risk a peep out, perhaps? Not yet; they might creep in.
A good hiding-place, this: the best you've ever found.
It's funny, though, they haven't tried again.
Can't hear a thing. They must be miles away.
The dark damp smell of sand is thicker now.
Give them another call: *Yoo-hoo! Come and find me!*
But they are still elsewhere. They'll think you're clever,
And ask you where you hid. Don't tell them. Keep it secret.
It's cold in here. You can't hear anything.
But wait. Let them hunt a little longer;
Think of them frowning at each other:
Where can he be? We've looked all over.
Something tickles on your nose. Your legs are stiff.
Just a little longer and then creep out.
They're not coming back. You've tricked them properly.
All right. Push off the sacks. That's better.
Good to be rid of that unpleasant smell.
Out of the shed. *Hey! Here I am! I'm here!*
I've won the game! You couldn't find me!
The darkening garden watches. Nothing stirs.
The bushes hold their breath. The air is cold.
Yes, here you are, but where are they who sought you?
VERNON SCANNELL

Talking about the poem

1. How does Vernon Scannell gain the reader's attention at the beginning of the poem?
2. Describe how the poet makes the reader imagine the smells, sounds and feelings which would be experienced by someone hiding in the toolshed.
3. How does the poet suggest the excitement in the voice of the hidden person?
4. Why does the hidden person feel proud of himself?
5. What makes the person feel relieved at first when he leaves the shed?
6. Why is he disappointed?
7. How is the ending of the poem made mysterious?

Writing your own poem

Imagine that you are blind. A friend accompanies you to a street market, or a covered market, and leads you around it, stopping to buy goods at various stalls. Use your sense of smell to recognise the stalls you are passing by or stopping at. Write a poem describing your tour of the market and its smells, trying to present the smells as vividly as possible. Remember, *read* and *revise* before copying out your final version.

Statements, questions and commands

In unit 1 we saw that there are three types of sentences: statements, questions and commands.

The sacks in the toolshed smell like the seaside. (a statement)
What's that? (a question)
Don't breathe or move. (a command)

We noted that statements end with full stops.

A question always ends with a question mark:
What is that?

A command ends with a full stop except when it is said sharply or loudly. Then it ends with an exclamation mark:
Go away!
Look out!
Come and find me!

A statement which is spoken sharply or loudly also ends with an exclamation mark:
Here I am!
I've won the game! You couldn't find me!

Exercise 1

The following sentences include statements and questions. Rewrite them, punctuating them correctly. Remember to begin each sentence with a capital letter.

1. what was that sound
2. it was only the wind in the trees
3. how can you be so sure
4. did you think it was something else
5. i do not know where it was coming from
6. you are scared far too easily, aren't you
7. perhaps you should take my fears more seriously
8. do you want me to look around outside
9. that would be safer, wouldn't it
10. it won't be safer if there really is something lurking in the darkness

Cold cloth and frozen buttons

The shirt was made of cold cloth and frozen buttons. It lay on Ainsley's bed like a drift of snow. The cold spring wind blew the curtains and moaned under the door. Ainsley stroked the shirt. It had been starched with ice.

'Are you ready?' said Mother from downstairs.

'Are you ready, Ainsley?' said Alice from her room next door. She was ready. She was always ready.

Ainsley picked up the shirt and shook it, but that only added more cold air to it. He dropped it again and sat on it, hoping to crack the chill. It was cold again by the time he had it over his head and it touched his skin. The warm clothes he had worn all day lay on the bed. He picked up his pullover and put his face in it, to warm his skin. The cold water he had washed with five minutes ago was still damp in front of his ears.

Alice rattled his door. Ainsley put his tie on and knotted it. It pulled his collar against his neck and took the heat from that. A big shiver organised itself and spread from his throat down to his feet. It made his shoes kick his ankles, because he was still sitting on the bed, and his feet were off the ground like a puppet's.

Alice was still rattling. Ainsley unlaced one shoe and then the next, and shook them off his feet. Then he tramped his trousers down on to the floor, and took the Sunday ones from the chair. They were as cold as glass too. A shiver went from his knees to the back of his neck. Then he put his jacket on, and clamped the shirt down on all the skin that had so far avoided the cold. He felt himself creeping. He had shivered his bones loose now. All he could do was shake his shoulders.

Alice was at the bottom of the stairs, pulling on a thin pair of gloves. She picked up her prayer book. Ainsley shut his bedroom door against the wind and set it moaning again. Alice looked at her watch and decided that they were not late yet. Ainsley came down and began to put his coat on.

'When will you be ready?' said Alice. 'When?'

'Now,' said Ainsley.

WILLIAM MAYNE *Sand*

Talking about the passage

1 What details and comparisons emphasise the coldness?
2 How did the cold affect Ainsley?
3 What kind of person is Alice?

Writing about the passage

1. How did Ainsley try to warm his shirt?
2. Why did Alice rattle his door?
3. What was the effect upon Ainsley when he put on his tie?
4. Why did Ainsley feel even colder when he put on his jacket?
5. What sound was heard when Ainsley closed his bedroom door?
6. How was Alice different from Ainsley in the way she behaved?
7. How do you try to overcome the effects of cold on winter days?

Openings

An over-used opening to a story always discourages your reader. It is a mistake to begin in a familiar way, that shows little thought, for example:

Once upon a time . . .
It was a lovely day. The sun was shining and the birds were singing.
The scene is . . .

It is far more effective to open a story by plunging straight into the action, without even setting the scene. This often demands the use of dialogue. The scene will become clearer as the action continues. Beginning in this way is a further example of appealing to the senses, as we imagine the sounds of distinctive voices.

Study the following openings carefully, and discuss how effective they are in gaining the readers' attention. Note that the sentence containing the words of any new speaker begins on a new line.

1 'Hey Mum, do you know what?'
   No answer.
   'Hey, Mum.'
   No answer.
   'MUM.'
   Sam bellowed with the full force of his lungs. His face turned red as a plum.
   'I'm not deaf, dear. There's no need to shout.'
                    NINA BAWDEN   *The White Horse Gang*

2 'Me wear a collar?' said Mason Ross, sitting up in bed and fingering the hard thing his mother had put into his hands. 'Give

up, Mam, it's not Sunday, and I don't want a collar for work. Folk don't work with collars on.'
                                        WILLIAM MAYNE   *The Incline*

3   This is the story of how we became a gang of thieves. My sister Jinny says I shouldn't start like this, giving away the story in the first sentence, but I think she's wrong. If you're writing a book, you've got to make sure the right sort of people read it, haven't you? Otherwise it's not fair to them or to you. So I'm starting off by saying this is a book about thieves and robbers so that no one who would rather read about fairies or magic or talking animals need bother to go any further. It's about me and my friends and how we turned thieves and brought a criminal to justice.
                                NINA BAWDEN   *A Handful of Thieves*

4   'Where is he?'
   Barney hopped from one foot to the other as he clambered down from the train, peering in vain through the white-faced crowds flooding eagerly to the St Austell ticket barrier. 'Oh, I can't see him. Is he there?'
                                SUSAN COOPER   *Over Sea, Under Stone*

5   'Too many!' James shouted, and slammed the door behind him.
   'What?' said Will.
   'Too many kids in this family, that's what. Just *too many*.'
                                SUSAN COOPER   *The Dark is Rising*

6   'Go now,' the dying man said. 'Take Harry and go – now, now . . .'
   Edmund held his father's hand and asked 'Where?'
                              BARBARA WILLARD   *Harrow and Harvest*

After discussing the extracts, write opening paragraphs for three stories with the following titles:

1   Runaway
2   The coming of the fair
3   The autumn morning

Try to make the openings different in style. Remember that each start should gain your reader's attention and make him or her want to read on.

Nouns

A *noun* is a word which gives a name to something or someone. Usually the name is for something that we see such as a person, a place, an animal or an object. The words in **heavy print** in the sentences below are all nouns.

*The **sky** is blue.*
*The **horse** lives in a **stable**.*
*The **lady** and the **man** have gone to the **cinema**.*

1. Make a list of nouns which name objects that you can see around you in a classroom.
2. Make a list of nouns which name pieces of furniture that you might find in a house.

Exercise 2

Rewrite the following sentences, underlining all the nouns which they include.

1. The boy decided to climb a tree.
2. The girl was horrified to see that the cup was broken.
3. The cat jumped down from the wall.
4. The torch floated down the river.
5. Round the corner came a coach.
6. The town was famous for its castle.
7. The shop has a new manager.
8. Grass grew around the statue.
9. Over the hill came a rider.
10. The mountain had never been climbed.

Exercise 3

Rewrite the following passage, underlining all the nouns.

Tea was about to begin. The table was set with plates, glasses, knives, forks and spoons. A serviette was neatly folded on each plate. There were two dishes containing sandwiches, and a large plate filled with buns. A cake waited, with its ten candles. Jelly and trifle stood on the sideboard. Steam rose from the spout of the teapot. The children hurried to their chairs.

Nouns which are general terms are called *common nouns*. 'A man' could name any man, 'a city' any city, 'an ocean' any ocean, and 'a ship' any ship.

Names of particular people, places and things are called *proper nouns*. 'Charles Dickens' was a particular man, 'London' is a particular city, the 'Pacific Ocean' is a particular ocean, and the 'Titanic' was a particular ship. Proper nouns always begin with capital letters.

Exercise 4

Rewrite the following sentences, putting in capital letters wherever they are needed.

1. last august sarah went to germany for a holiday.
2. she took the ferry that left harwich and crossed the north sea.
3. the ship, the "queen juliana", docked at the hook of holland.
4. sarah travelled by car through holland, passing the towns of rotterdam and arnhem.
5. at the end of the long journey, she arrived at burgdorf, a town near hanover.
6. she stayed with her penfriend, helga schmidt, who had a dog called heidi.
7. sarah found german very difficult to understand.
8. during her stay she visited the harz mountains, which are near the east german border.
9. the holiday was in august, and it is now october, but sarah remembers it clearly.
10. next year she would like to go across the channel to france and, perhaps, travel to italy so that she can see rome.

Letter-writing

Letters are used to convey information to a person or to a group of people. In this section you will be shown how to set out a letter to a friend, but remember that what you say in the letter, and the way in which you say it, are far more important than the layout.

Envelopes and postcards, must be addressed clearly and correctly. Why?

This is a correctly addressed envelope:

```
                                    [stamp]

        John Phillips,
           108 Crossfields Avenue,
        BRIXHAM,
           Devon.
              BR1 1OR
```

Notice how the address is punctuated and indented, and also notice that no abbreviations should be used in the address. Why is the town in capital letters? Why are capital letters used at the beginning of the other words in the address?

A letter to a friend is set out like this:

```
                              'Drury Cottage,'
                              12 Priory Lane,
                              Ripon,
                              North Yorkshire.
                              RP2 3BT
                              22nd October, 1983.

Dear Jim,
         As it has been so long since I last
wrote to you, I thought
```

```
Let me know as soon as possible whether you
will be able to come.
            Yours sincerely,
                    Anne Jones.
```

You can see that the address is set out and punctuated as on the envelope, except that the town is no longer written in capital letters. The date should be written in full.

There is a comma after 'Dear Jim', but the next word, 'As', begins with a capital letter. The main part of the letter begins on a new line. The first word of the ending, 'Yours sincerely', begins on a new line with a capital letter, and the expression is followed by a comma before your signature on the line below.

Letters to friends need not end with the words 'Yours sincerely'. Amongst the other possible endings are 'Yours', 'Sincerely yours', 'Your friend' and 'With love from'.

Draw an envelope, and set out this address correctly putting in capital letters wherever they are needed:

shirley waterman 19 seaview road weymouth dorset we4 1ef

Set out and punctuate the following letter correctly. Remember that the address and date should contain no abbreviations, and that all proper nouns begin with capital letters.

15 cathedral ave salisbury wiltshire sa3 2lo 21/11/83
dear shirley i wonder if you would like to come and stay at my house next weekend. sally barlow is holding her birthday party then and has asked me to invite you. it would also give us a chance to visit the wiltshire horse show on saturday and watch the jumping.
could you please bring some of your records as i would like to tape them on a cassette i received for my birthday last month.
i hope you can come. please drop me a line to let me know with love from pat

A letter to a penfriend

What is a penfriend? Perhaps you already have one. If you do not, and you would like one, it might be possible to arrange a link with another school, in a different part of the country, or even in another country. It can be very interesting for a class to exchange letters with a class in another school.

Write an introductory letter to a penfriend. If this is a letter which can really be sent, so much the better. Before you start discuss what has to be included in a first letter. It would help to put yourself in the place of the person who is going to receive the letter. What would he or she want to know about you? Plan your letter by writing notes on what you are going to say.

Further reading

Nina Bawden's novels are set in the British Isles, and usually involve adventures by children. Her best-known works, all available in paperback, are:

Carrie's War
Carrie and her brother Nick are evacuated from London to Wales during the Second World War. They live with Mr Evans, of whom they are rather afraid, and his timid sister. The children's friend, Albert, lives with Hepzibah Green and the strange Mister Johnny at Druid's Bottom, until desire for revenge makes Carrie do a terrible thing!

A Handful of Thieves
Mr Gribble disappears with Gran's savings. Fred with his friends on the Cemetery Committee decide to track Gribble down. This involves a thrilling and dangerous chase.

On the Run
Ben Mallory is staying with his father and stepmother-to-be in London. He befriends Thomas, the son of an East African Prime Minister. With Lit, who is on the run from 'the Welfare', Ben helps Thomas evade his father's political enemies.

The Peppermint Pig
Poll and Theo are going through difficulties but are cheered by the activities of Johnnie, a little pig, who is not only naughty but very clever.

The Robbers
When Philip leaves his grandmother and the castle by the sea to visit his father and stepmother in London, he expects the worst. But then he meets Darcy, from the other side of the canal, and life becomes almost too exciting!

The Runaway Summer
Mary's parents are getting divorced. Mary is unhappy and unpleasant, but when she is sent to stay with her grandfather and Aunt Alice she meets Simon, a policeman's son. Together they help an illegal immigrant boy, Krishna, to find his uncle and outwit the police.

Squib
Squib is a shy small boy in a park. He is a mystery. Kate tries to discover who Squib is and in doing so gets into a terrifying situation.

The White Horse Gang
The gang plot to kidnap a small boy, but being kidnappers involves lots of problems!

The Witch's Daughter
Perdita frightens all the children but when Tim and his blind sister, Janey, arrive from the mainland with the strange Mr Jones, Perdita becomes involved in an exciting mystery.

3 Writing about animals

In unit 1 we emphasised the importance of careful observation to your writing about places. It is also essential to watch animals closely when you want to write about them.

Almost everyone has the opportunity to observe living creatures that are wild. Even if you live in a city centre there are wild birds to be seen, and they can be fascinating to watch. The details that you notice will help you to bring realistic creatures into your stories.

If you have a pet you will have seen that all creatures are different: they are all individuals. If you bring out the special characteristics of each animal your writing will be much more effective.

Bubble and Squeak

As her daughter had two gerbils, Philippa Pearce was able to write very convincingly about these animals in The Battle of Bubble and Squeak. *Sid, Peggy and Amy have never owned a pet before and they are given two gerbils, much against the wishes of their mother, Mrs Sparrow.*

Sid may not have loved his gerbils in the way that Peggy did, but he was conscientious about them. He changed their food and water daily, and cleaned out their cage every weekend. He exercised them often. What they seemed to enjoy was the freedom of a limitless plain – the living-room table would do – with a great many tunnels. To begin with, the children made the tunnels out of newspaper rolled up, with rubber bands to keep the rolling-up in place. Then they began to collect the cardboard inner tubes of toilet rolls from the lavatory and of kitchen rolls from the kitchen. The longer tubes were kept for the table; and the shorter ones went straight into the cage.

Besides using the tubes as runways, the gerbils gnawed them to bits. If they didn't gnaw cardboard, they gnawed the bars of the cage or of the restored treadmill. The cardboard they gnawed filled the cage with cardboard crumbs, and the crumbs pushed themselves out through the bars of the cage on to the table or the floor; so did the gerbil bedding. Someone had to clear up the mess. After that first night's experience, Mrs Sparrow refused to do any more

clearing up after gerbils. Sid did it. He used the vacuum cleaner regularly nowadays. He did not object. He rather enjoyed the job of emptying the cleaner. Once it went wrong, and he mended it.

'You can't say he doesn't work at it,' said Bill Sparrow. 'You might do worse than keep those gerbils, you know.'

'You're soft,' said Alice Sparrow. 'I don't like them. I don't *trust* them.'

It turned out that she was right not to trust them.

The gerbil cage was kept on the living-room table, until the table was needed. Then Sid or Peggy would lift the cage on to the wide window-sill. When the table was clear again, the cage was put back. But sometimes, of course, the children forgot to do that. It did not seem to matter much if the gerbils stayed on the window-sill, anyway. There was even room, after dark, to draw the curtains across the window, between the back of the cage and the window itself.

The curtains were rather handsome scarlet ones that Mrs Sparrow had made herself. When they were drawn behind the cage, their folds brushed against the bars at the back.

      PHILIPPA PEARCE *The Battle of Bubble and Squeak*

Talking about the passage

1 What does the reader learn about the gerbils from reading this passage?
2 Why did Mrs Sparrow not like the gerbils?
3 Can you guess why it *did* matter if the gerbils stayed on the window-sill?
4 Were the gerbils suitable pets for the three children?
5 Which pets would have given least trouble to Mrs Sparrow?

Writing about the passage

1 How do we know that Sid looked after the gerbils carefully?
2 What did he do to exercise Bubble and Squeak?
3 In which two ways did the gerbils make a mess on the table?
4 How did Sid clear up the mess?
5 Why did Bill Sparrow think that the gerbils might be good for Sid?
6 What caused the children to move the cage on to the window-sill sometimes?
7 Why were the curtains important to Mrs Sparrow?
8 Why was it unwise to leave the cage on the window-sill?

Writing instructions

Sid, Peggy and Amy find themselves in trouble because they have not had enough advice on how to look after their gerbils. Choose one particular pet which you know or which you can find out about, and write instructions on how to look after it, under the following headings:

1 Buying the pet
2 What to feed it on
3 A place to sleep
4 Exercising your pet
5 Keeping it clean
6 Special things to remember

Make sure that any reader would find your instructions clear and simple.

Take one home for the kiddies

On shallow straw, in shadeless glass,
Huddled by empty bowls they sleep;
No dark, no dam, no earth, no grass –
'Mam, get us one of them to keep.'

Living toys are something novel,
But it soon wears off somehow.
Fetch the shoebox, fetch the shovel –
'Mam, we're playing funerals now.'

PHILIP LARKIN

Talking about the poem

1 How does the poet want us to feel towards the animals?
2 What do we learn of the way creatures are kept in a pet shop?
3 Why do the children in the poem want pets?
4 How do the children's feelings change after a while?
5 Is the poet fair in the way he presents children?
6 Why do you think the poet wrote the poem?

Writing your own poem

Look carefully at the dog in the picture. Why is it there? Who owns it? How does it feel?

Write a poem describing its thoughts about its life. After you have completed your rough draft, revise it carefully and then make a final copy.

Nouns

In unit 2 we discussed nouns, and said that they usually name things that we can see. This is not always the case. Some nouns name things which can be heard or smelt:
She heard the **laughter.**
He smelled the **gas.**

Other nouns name feelings, such as 'coldness'. Some name qualities, like 'kindness', and other things which cannot be recognised by the senses, such as 'conscience'.

Exercise 1

Write out the following sentences, underlining all the nouns which they contain.

1 It often showed its ferocity.
2 She was filled with sorrow when it died.
3 All of it had vanished from his memory.
4 His jealousy ended their friendship.
5 Her happiness could be seen by everyone.
6 They were given their freedom.
7 The warmth made them feel contented.
8 That thought did not lessen their fear.
9 It showed its courage and cunning.
10 The coldness caused their misery.

Letter-writing

At half-term, in October, you are invited to stay with a cousin who lives on a farm. During your stay write a letter home describing the holiday and the animals you have seen, concentrating on one in particular.

Make a note of the material that you mean to include. Take care to choose language that suits your readers. How should the letter be set out? How should it start? How should it end?

When you have finished your rough draft, read it through, asking yourself how interesting your readers will find it. When you have made any necessary improvements, copy out your final version.

Pussy

Although pets are a great responsibility they can also be of great value. In the next passage a family is moving to a new estate from an area that is being demolished. They are all anxious about going. When they are about to leave, Jean, aged eight, is found to be missing. She has recently taken in a stray cat, and her father has told her that she cannot take it to their new home. Kevin and Sandra go to look for her with Mr Hedley, a neighbour, and find Jean in a ruined house.

Quietly Sandra and I crept in through the open doorway. On the rubble-strewn floor of what had been the living-room a battered grey cat with scarred face and torn ear crouched over the open catfood tin. He looked up suspiciously as we entered, and when I made a slight move towards him he slunk into a corner.

'You've interrupted his dinner!' cried Jean indignantly; and then, addressing the cat in the same tender voice as before: 'Poor old Pussy, did they frighten you? Never mind, they're not going to hurt my Pussy. Now finish your meal, like a good cat.'

'Fancy buying that stuff at a shilling a tin!' I remarked. 'Haven't you anything better to do with your money?'

'It was my shilling,' said Jean defiantly. 'A lady gave me it for an errand. I can spend it how I like. That's right, Pussy, you eat it up.'

Warily Pussy returned to the open tin and went on eating, though ready to retreat at any moment.

'Come on, folks!' called Mr Hedley from the street outside. 'Time we were on our way!'

'Pussy can't come just yet,' said Jean. 'Not till he's finished.'

'Pussy can't come at all,' I said.

'But I want him,' said Jean. 'I want him to love. That's what I want him for.'

'He'll have to be put to sleep,' I said.

Jean clenched her fists.

'I'm not going to Westwood without Pussy!' she declared. And then, softening her voice to speak to the cat: 'There, there, pet, come to your mum!'

Pussy had finished eating, and now he let Jean pick him up, though he was still eyeing the rest of us with a good deal of suspicion.

'It's no good, duck,' said Mr Hedley. 'You couldn't do with 'im at Westwood. Anyroad, 'e probably wouldn't go with you, or if 'e did, 'e wouldn't stay. Cats gets attached to their own 'omes.'

'Of course he'd come with me!' said Jean.

Sandra hadn't spoken since we arrived at the empty house. She was in one of her thoughtful moods.

'Bring him as far as the van, anyway,' she said to Jean, 'and see what happens. But you know what your dad said last time!'

And then, turning to us, Sandra added quietly:

'Poor kid, it's quite true, she wants something to love. And we'll have plenty of problems at Westwood anyway. A cat more or less won't make much difference.'

JOHN ROWE TOWNSEND *Widdershins Crescent*

Talking about the passage

1 Why did Kevin think that Jean was wrong to feed the cat?
2 How suitable was the name 'Pussy' for this cat?
3 What made Jean want to keep Pussy?
4 How did Mr Hedley try to comfort Jean?

Writing about the passage

1 Describe the cat in your own words.
2 How did the cat behave when Kevin moved towards it?
3 Why was Jean annoyed with Kevin and Sandra?
4 How could Jean afford to buy catfood?
5 What did Kevin think should happen to Pussy?
6 Why, according to Mr Hedley, would it be pointless to try to take Pussy to the new house?
7 Why did Sandra say that Jean could take the cat to the van?
8 What do children gain from having pets?

The end

In unit 2 you were shown how to begin a story so that your reader's attention was caught from the start. Once you have his or her attention you should try to keep it until the last word has been read. Even then your story should leave the reader thinking. You might choose to end on a mysterious note, with a strong suggestion of the mood left by the story, or you might choose to finish your story at the very moment that the action is completed. You might leave your reader with a vivid sense impression – a memorable picture or a haunting sound.

Just as there are over-used starts, so there are over-used endings. Stories frequently end in one of the following ways:
. . . and then I woke up. It had all been a dream.
I went home and had my tea, and then I went to bed.
Such endings usually appear suddenly, when the writer has run out of ideas or interest.

The following passages are the endings of four short stories. Read them and then discuss the feelings and thoughts with which the writer seems to want to leave his readers.

1   He did not move. Eyes shut, he waited, shivering. He heard Travis breathe loud in the room; he heard Travis shift his rifle, click the safety catch, and raise the weapon.

There was a sound of thunder.

RAY BRADBURY   *A Sound of Thunder*

2   After walking away at last he turned and looked back. She was walking back to the house, pressing her body against the wind and at the same time gazing down at the earth. He halted a moment in the hope that she would turn round, but nothing happened and he went on.

When he turned again she had disappeared altogether and nothing moved against the dead little house except the high sunless poplars beaten by the sea-wind.

H E BATES   *Time to Kill*

3   My own mistake arose, naturally enough, through too careless, too inquisitive, and too impulsive a temperament. But of late, it is a rare thing that I sleep soundly at night. There is a countenance which haunts me, turn as I will. There is an hysterical laugh which will for ever ring within my ears.

EDGAR ALLAN POE   *The Oblong Box*

4 'Wish me luck!' cried Willie.

'Best of luck, son,' called the porter, waving, smiling. 'Best of luck, boy!'

'Thanks,' said Willie, in the great sound of the train, in the steam and roar.

He watched the black train until it was completely gone away and out of sight. He did not move all the time it was going. He stood quietly, a small boy twelve years old, on the worn wooden platform, and only after three entire minutes did he turn at last to face the empty streets below.

Then, as the sun was rising, he began to walk very fast, so as to keep warm, down into the new town.

RAY BRADBURY *Hail and Farewell*

Before you begin to write a story you should be certain of how it will end.

Write a story that closes with *one* of the following endings:

1 The footsteps stopped outside. A face peered in. 'I've found it,' said a voice.
2 She stood motionless, listening to the fading hoofbeats.
3 On the floor lay a single, glistening feather.

Commas

When you are writing a list of words or phrases, the individual words or phrases should be separated by commas.

She fed carrots, cabbage, lettuce and grain to her rabbit.
The rabbit was young, white and fluffy.
The pet shop sold white mice, golden hamsters, puppies and kittens.

If the last two items on the list are joined by 'and', you do not usually put a comma before the word 'and'.

Exercise 2

Rewrite the following sentences, putting in commas wherever they are needed.

1 Rosemary put on her boots a thick cardigan her anorak and a warm scarf.

2   She had decided to take her young excitable and energetic dog for a run on the beach.
3   In autumn the beach was exciting because the sea was rough dangerous and threatening.
4   There were no castles moats sandpies or drawings left by children on the beach.
5   The sands were marked by birds' feet dogs' paws and the shoes of an occasional stroller.
6   The beach was not littered with paper-bags orange peel lollipop-sticks and empty cans.
7   Rosemary's dog sniffed the pieces of wood festoons of seaweed starfish and dead crabs that lay along the water's edge.
8   Rosemary climbed the wooden steps that were rickety worn and bleached by the sea.
9   On the promenade she tried to peer into a kiosk with news-

paper over its windows a large padlock on the door and a sign that said, 'To let'.
10 She walked home past closed shops that looked drab without their bright awnings racks of postcards and heaps of toys for sale.

Writing your own poem

Look carefully at the contrasting pictures of cats. Notice the characters brought out by the photographers. Write a poem bringing out the differences between the cat on a beach and the cat outside in the darkness. In particular try to bring out the way in which the cat moves, and notice the details of its appearance.

Using a dictionary

It is extremely useful to have a dictionary with you whenever you are writing or reading. We know the meanings of many words which we never use when we write, perhaps because we are unsure of their spelling or precise meaning. Using a dictionary to check spelling and meaning helps us to use exactly the word we need.

If you meet a new word it is best to look up its meaning at once, and to learn it. You might find it valuable to keep a list of such words, in a notebook or at the back of your exercise book.

In completing the punctuation exercise above, you may not have known the meanings of 'festoons', 'kiosks' and 'awnings'. If so, you should have looked up the words in a dictionary.

Remember that a dictionary has its words arranged in alphabetical order.

Rearrange each of the following groups of nouns in the order you would expect to find them in a dictionary:

1 promenade, stroller, anorak, kiosk, padlock, starfish, festoon, cardigan, awning, postcard.
2 awning, anorak, avenue, account, application, archery, abolition, ailment, aeroplane, astronomy.
3 festoon, fence, festival, fetlock, ferret, federation, feast, fever, fetter, feature.

If you looked up the word 'awning', you would find this entry in a dictionary:
awning, *n.* a covering to shelter from the sun or weather.
The letter *n.* shows that 'awning' is a noun.

If you looked up 'festoon', you would find:
festoon, *n.* garland.

For each of these words only one meaning is given, but some words have more than one meaning. If you looked up the word 'kiosk' you might read:
kiosk, *n.* an Eastern garden pavilion; a small out-of-doors roofed stall for sale of papers, sweets, etc.; a bandstand; a public telephone box.

Then you have to compare the possible meanings with the way the word is used in the sentence being read. Perhaps the sentence is:
On the promenade Rosemary tried to peer into a kiosk with newspaper over its

windows, a large padlock on the door and a sign that said, 'To let'.
As Rosemary is on a promenade, 'kiosk', in this case, cannot mean 'an Eastern garden pavilion'. Nor can it mean 'a bandstand', as a bandstand would not have windows and a door. If it were 'a public telephone box', it would not be 'To let'. Therefore, the most likely meaning for 'kiosk' in this sentence, is 'a small out-of-doors roofed stall'.

Vocabulary

A dictionary usually tells you the origin of a word, as well as its meaning. If you looked up 'cardigan' you would find,
cardigan, *n.* a knitted woollen jacket, named after Lord Cardigan (1797–1868).

The following nouns all come from the names of people. Use a dictionary to find out how these words originated:
boycott, dahlia, guillotine, loganberry, lynching, macadam, mesmerism, sandwich, silhouette, wellingtons.

Further reading

Philippa Pearce was the daughter of a miller, whose mill stood on the River Cam at Great Shelford in Cambridgeshire. The river ran beside the mill house garden and then under the mill, which it partly powered. Philippa Pearce uses the village, the river and the countryside as a realistic background in many of her books. These include:

Tom's Midnight Garden
Tom is lonely and angry in an old, dull house in the Fens, but there he finds adventure. At midnight he discovers a garden; a garden of his dreams? There, too, is Hatty, an orphan girl. Hatty and the garden contain a mystery.

A Dog So Small
Ben longs for his own dog but he lives in a London backstreet which is not suitable for a dog. His birthday present from his grandfather was only a woodcut picture of a small dog. However, Ben thought, 'What about a dog so small you could see it only with your eyes shut?'

What the Neighbours Did and Other Stories
Eight humorous stories about ordinary people, including the family blackberry trip run by Dad, the midnight feast and 'what the neighbours did'.

Minnow on the Say
An exciting story of a treasure hunt in a river setting based on the writer's home area.

4 Christmas

Christmas is one of the most exciting parts of the school year with many concerts and plays being put on by pupils and teachers. It has also inspired many writers. In this unit we are going to look at some of the traditional aspects of Christmas.

It is useful to pause here and stress some of the advice which you have already been given.

- Always remember to think of the readers for whom your work is intended.
- Be critical of your own writing and try hard to improve it.
- Describe places, events and animals in detail.
- Use your senses to make your work convincing.

It is particularly important to make your setting realistic when you are writing a fantasy, like *The Wind in the Willows*.

The carol-singers

Mole invited Rat into his home, which he had left some time before. Mole was upset at finding so little to eat there, but Rat cheered him up and prepared a sparse meal.

At last the Rat succeeded in decoying him to the table, and had just got seriously to work with the sardine-opener when sounds were heard from the fore-court without – sounds like the scuffling of small feet in the gravel and a confused murmur of tiny voices, while broken sentences reached them – 'Now, all in a line – hold the lantern up a bit, Tommy – clear your throats first – no coughing after I say one, two, three. – Where's young Bill? – Here, come on, do, we're all a-waiting –'

'What's up?' inquired the Rat, pausing in his labours.

'I think it must be the field-mice,' replied the Mole, with a touch of pride in his manner. 'They go round carol-singing regularly at this time of the year. They're quite an institution in these parts. And they never pass me over – they come to Mole End last of all; and I used to give them hot drinks, and supper too sometimes, when I could afford it. It will be like old times to hear them again.'

'Let's have a look at them!' cried the Rat, jumping up and running to the door.

It was a pretty sight, and a seasonable one, that met their eyes when they flung the door open. In the fore-court, lit by the dim rays of a horn lantern, some eight or ten little field-mice stood in a semi-circle, red worsted comforters round their throats, their forepaws thrust deep into their pockets, their feet jigging for warmth. With bright beady eyes they glanced shyly at each other, sniggering a little, sniffing and applying coat-sleeves a good deal. As the door opened, one of the elder ones that carried the lantern was just saying, 'Now then, one, two, three!' and forthwith their shrill little voices uprose on the air, singing one of the old-time carols that their forefathers composed in fields that were fallow and held by frost, or when snow-bound in chimney corners, and handed down to be sung in the miry street to lamp-lit windows at Yule-time.

Carol

> Villagers all, this frosty tide,
> Let your doors swing open wide,
> Though wind may follow, and snow beside,
> Yet draw us in by your fire to bide;
>   Joy shall be yours in the morning!

> Here we stand in the cold and the sleet,
> Blowing fingers and stamping feet,
> Come from far away you to greet –
> You by the fire and we in the street –
>   Bidding you joy in the morning!
>
> For ere one half of the night was gone,
> Sudden a star has led us on,
> Raining bliss and benison –
> Bliss to-morrow and more anon,
>   Joy for every morning!
>
> Goodman Joseph toiled through the snow –
> Saw the star o'er a stable low;
> Mary she might not further go –
> Welcome thatch, and litter below!
>   Joy was hers in the morning!
>
> And then they heard the angels tell
> 'Who were the first to cry Nowell?
> Animals all, as it befell,
> In the stable where they did dwell!
>   Joy shall be theirs in the morning!'

  The voices ceased, the singers, bashful but smiling, exchanged sidelong glances, and silence succeeded – but for a moment only. Then, from up above and far away, down the tunnel they had so lately travelled was borne to their ears in a faint musical hum the sound of distant bells ringing a joyful and clangorous peal.

  'Very well sung, boys!' cried the Rat heartily. 'And now come along in, all of you, and warm yourselves by the fire, and have something hot!'

                KENNETH GRAHAME   *The Wind in the Willows*

Talking about the passage

1. How is the excitement and nervousness of the singers suggested by the author?
2. Why did Mole feel proud that the carol-singers had arrived?
3. Why is the carol unusual?
4. How are the animals given human characteristics?
5. Which words has the writer used to suggest sounds?
6. How does the writer make the reader use his or her senses?

Writing about the passage

1. What were the first signs of the carol-singers' arrival?
2. How did Mole know that the singers were the field-mice?
3. Why was he pleased that they had come?
4. Describe the appearance of the field-mice.
5. How did they try to keep warm?
6. When was the carol composed, and by whom?
7. Kenneth Grahame has chosen to use some old-fashioned words in this passage. Find out the meanings of the following: comforters, forthwith, bide, benison.
8. How do you feel about carol-singers calling?
9. Describe the aspects of Christmas which seem to you to be most important.

Writing a story

Kenneth Grahame writes about animals with many human characteristics. They think and talk as humans do, yet they are still obviously animals.

 Choose a particular creature and describe its Christmas Day. What you write will be fantasy so you need to use a realistic, detailed setting. Before you start, imagine your creatures and their characters. Think of the various aspects of a human's Christmas Day and decide what would be the animal's version of such things as the Christmas tree, presents, dinner, cards and carols. Make sure that your story has an interesting beginning and end.

Commas

When a sentence is interrupted, commas are used around the interruption. It might be one word, such as 'however'.
*The card, **however**, should arrive on time.*

 If the interruption delays the start or end of the sentence, one comma is enough to cut off the interruption.
***However**, the card should arrive on time.*
*The card should arrive on time, **however**.*

 Sometimes the interruption is a word or phrase added to provide an explanation or description.

*My brother, **Derek**, is coming home for Christmas.*
*Rover, **the dog we bought last Friday**, attacked the postman.*

Exercise 1

Rewrite the following sentences, including commas wherever they are needed.

1. Jennifer an old friend visited me on Saturday.
2. The Christmas tree covered in lights and tinsel stood in the corner.
3. Nevertheless the nativity play was very enjoyable.
4. The paper red with green patterns was wrapped neatly around the present.
5. I bought my sisters Jane and Elizabeth gloves for Christmas.
6. The family however was not at home when we called.
7. One envelope large and brown contained a calendar.
8. The guests moreover had already begun to arrive.
9. Evergreens holly and ivy were used to decorate the church.
10. The carol service is still to take place fortunately.

Wassailers

Carol-singers are a familiar aspect of Christmas, but carols were sung long before Jesus was born. Carols were once songs which accompanied dances. The singing dancers or 'wassailers' who went round ancient pagan villages at midwinter were thought to bring good luck. Winter was a time of hunger, and a feast encouraged people as they faced a long shortage of food. The great fires of the midwinter feast were intended to show that the cold and darkness would not last for ever, and that the sun would regain its power in the spring, bringing growth and a rich harvest. Evergreen plants, such as holly, were taken as a reminder of the greenness which would eventually return to the earth. Some old carols, sung by the wassailers, recall the pagan beliefs, such as this one:

Here we come a-wassailing among the leaves so green.
Here we come a-wandering so fairly to be seen.
   Now is winter-time, strangers travel far and near,
   And we wish you and send you a happy New Year.

We hope that all your barley will prosper fine and grow,
So that you'll have plenty and a bit more to bestow.
   We hope your wethers they grow fat and likewise all your ewes,
   And where they had one lamb we hope they will have two.

Bud and blossom, bud and blossom, bud and bloom and bear,
So we may have plenty and cider all next year.
   Hatfuls and in capfuls and bushel-bags and all,
   And the cider running out of every gutter-hole.

Down here in the muddy lane there sits an old red fox,
Starving and a-shivering and licking his old chops.
   Bring us out your table and spread it if you please,
   And give us hungry wassailers a bit of bread and cheese.

I've a little purse and it's made of leather skin.
A little silver sixpence would line it well within.
   Now is winter-time, strangers travel far and near,
   And we wish you and send you a happy New Year.

A L LLOYD   Folk Song in England

Mummers' play

The idea of the earth seeming to die in winter and to be born again in spring also lies behind the ancient mummers' plays (folk plays) which used to be acted throughout England. Characters in the plays die, and are brought back to life by magic.

   The hero of the mummers' play is St George. His enemy is the Turkish Knight. Sometimes a dragon is also brought in to fight St George. The characters include Father Christmas, who announces that the play is starting and who has to clear a space for the actors (as the play was usually put on in rooms that had no stage). Magic is brought into the play by the Doctor with his unusual cures. The play ends with a procession of characters played by the rest of the mumming band.

   It is likely that mummers' plays were performed for thousands of years before they were first written down. They were remembered and passed on to the boys of each village. Sometimes the names of the characters were changed, and sometimes strange comments crept into the plays. (Why, for example, does St George call the Turkish Knight 'my father' in the play which follows?) The story, however, remained the same.

The following version of the mummers' play from Romsey, Hampshire, was written down about 1830, by John Latham. The play was acted every Christmas by young men whose clothes were decorated with coloured ribbons.

(Enter Father Christmas)
FATHER CHRISTMAS: Welcome, welcome old Father Christmas.
In comes old Father Christmas
Welcome or welcome not,
I hope old Father Christmas will never be forgot.
Rome, Rome I do disdain
For after comes St George and all his noble train,
and in this room there shall be shown
The finest battle that ever was known
Between St George and the Turkish Knight.

(Enter St George)
ST GEORGE: In come I St George, St George
That valiant man of courage bold,
All with my sword and spear I won ten crowns of gold.
I fought the fierce dragon and brought him to slaughter
and by this means I won the King of Bohemia's daughter.

(Enter the Turkish Knight)
TURKISH KNIGHT: In come I the Turkish Knight
to old England for the fight
I will fight St George that valiant man of courage bold
and if his blood is hot I'll quickly make it cold.

(They fight and St George vanquishes the Turkish Knight.)
ST GEORGE: I am a little man that talks very bold
much like a lad that I have been told.
Therefore draw out thy sword and fight, or pull out thy purse and pay –
Satisfaction I will have before I go away.
TURKISH KNIGHT: Spare me St George, and do not cut me down.
ST GEORGE: Oh, I'll cut thee down and thou shalt rise no more.
Then forfeit thy life to make a store.
Gentlemen and Ladies walk out and see what miracles I've done.
I've cut and slain my father down all by the evening sun.

                    Oh doctor, doctor! Is there an Italian doctor lately
                                              come from Spain
                    to heal the sick and raise the dead again?
                    Oh yes, there is an Italian doctor lately come from
                                                            Spain
                    to heal the sick and raise the dead again.
(Doctor appears)
                    Oh doctor, what canst thou cure?
DOCTOR: I can cure itch, pitch, palsy and gout
                    and raging pains that run both in and out,
                    broken legs and arms, if any man shall break his
                                                              neck
                    I will set it again, and have nothing for my pains.
ST GEORGE: Oh Doctor, what is thy pay?
DOCTOR: Ten guineas is my fee, but ten pounds I will take of
                                                             thee.
ST GEORGE: Take it –
DOCTOR: I've got a little bottle in the band of my breeches
                                                called Elecampane
(Applies it)
                    Rise, Beau Champion
                    and fight again.
(The Turkish Knight rises up)
TURKISH KNIGHT: The dragon is my enemy, to quietly end the strife
                    I'll crop his wings, he shall fly no more,
                    St George shall end his life.

(Enter Cut and Star)

CUT AND STAR: In come I, Cut and Star – just come from the bloody war.
I and seven more will beat eleven score.
Marching men of war, many battles I have seen,
many battles have I been in for St George, our king.

(Enter Poor and Mean)

POOR AND MEAN: In come I, Poor and Mean, hardly worthy to be seen.
Christmas comes but once a year.
When it comes it brings good cheer.
Roast beef, plum pudding and mince pie,
No-body loves them better than I.
A mug of Christmas ale will make us dance and sing
and money in our pockets is a very fine thing.

(Enter Bold Slasher)

BOLD SLASHER: In come I Bold Slasher, Bold Slasher is my name.
With my sword and buckler by my side I hope to win this game.
What man, what man comes under my bloody hand
I cut him and slay him as small as dust
and send him to the cook's shop to make pie crust.

(Enter Twing Twang)

TWING TWANG: In comes Twing Twang, Lieutenant of the press gang.*
I press all these bold mummers and send them aboard
a man-of-war – To fight the French and Dutch
and Spaniards also.

(Enter Jolly Jack)

JOLLY JACK: In come I, Jolly Jack, with my wife and children at my back,
When she comes she only says
Gentleman and ladies give me what you please.

(Exit all saying: I wish you a merry Christmas and a happy New Year,
A pocketful of money and a cellar full of beer.)

---

* The press gang was a group of sailors sent out to capture men to serve in the navy during the eighteenth and nineteenth centuries, when few men wished to join it.

For discussion

Imagine that your class is to put on a performance of the play.

- Where would you find a suitable place for the play to be performed?
- Who would form a suitable audience?
- How many actors should be involved?
- What costumes would you need?
- What stage properties would be required?
- How should the actors enter at the beginning and leave at the end?

Written work

Imagine that the play is to be performed for your parents and other pupils at your school.

1. Design a poster advertising the performance. What information is it necessary for the poster to give? How will you set out the information so that it is easy to understand? What kinds of lettering would be suitable? How will you make the poster attract attention?
2. Write the letter you would send to parents inviting them to see the play. How would you set out the letter? How would you begin and end it? What information should the letter include? How will you try to persuade the parents to come?

Carols

We have included examples of an animal carol and of a wassail song. These were probably new to you. *In the bleak mid-winter* is a very well-known carol, but you may never have looked closely at its words. Like most religious carols, it shows a writer taking the familiar Christmas story and trying to make you see it in a fresh way.

In the bleak mid-winter

In the bleak mid-winter
    Frosty wind made moan,

Earth stood hard as iron,
   Water like a stone;
Snow had fallen, snow on snow,
   Snow on snow,
In the bleak mid-winter
   Long ago.

Our God, Heaven cannot hold Him,
   Nor earth sustain;
Heaven and earth shall flee away
   When he comes to reign:
In the bleak mid-winter
   A stable-place sufficed
The Lord God Almighty
   Jesus Christ.

Enough for Him, whom cherubim
   Worship night and day,
A breastful of milk,
   And a mangerful of hay;
Enough for Him, whom angels
   Fall down before,
The ox and ass and camel
   Which adore.

Angels and archangels
   May have gathered there,
Cherubim and seraphim
   Thronged the air:
But only His mother
   In her maiden bliss
Worshipped the Belovèd
   With a kiss.

What can I give Him,
   Poor as I am?
If I were a shepherd
   I would bring a lamb;
If I were a wise man
   I would do my part;
Yet what can I give Him –
   Give my heart.

                  CHRISTINA GEORGINA ROSSETTI

Talking about the carol

1. How does Christina Rossetti make the midwinter seem bleak?
2. Why does she want midwinter in Palestine to seem like that?
3. How does she bring out the contrast between Jesus's importance and the way in which he was born?
4. What are archangels, cherubim and seraphim?
5. What present could a poor person, or a child, bring for Jesus?
6. Which side of the Christmas story does the writer emphasise?
7. How does the writer want us to feel?
8. Why do we not usually think about the words of carols?

Writing your own poem

Christmas is associated with many kinds of bells: the bells of churches and cathedrals; doorbells rung by carol-singers and postmen; the small bells decorating Christmas trees; the bells on cash registers; bells pictured on cards; the sleigh bells children listen for on Christmas Eve.

Are there any other bells you associate with Christmas?

What are the sounds made by the various bells, and which words best suggest these sounds? How are you affected by the different kinds of bells?

Write a poem called 'Christmas bells', describing some of these bells, their sounds, and the thoughts and feelings they arouse in you.

Writing a story

In The Return of the Native, *Thomas Hardy describes a performance of a mummers' play. After rehearsing, the mummers put on their costumes, decorated with ribbons and pieces of silk, and walked through the dark countryside to act their play at an inn.*

There was a slight hoar-frost that night, and the moon, though not more than half full, threw a spirited and enticing brightness upon the fantastic figures of the mumming band, whose plumes and ribbons rustled in their walk like autumn leaves. Their path was not over Rainbarrow now, but down a valley which left that ancient elevation a little to the east. The bottom of the vale was green to a width of ten yards or thereabouts, and the shining facets of frost upon the blades of grass seemed to move on with the shadows of those they surrounded. The masses of furze and heath to the right and left were dark as ever; a mere half-moon was powerless to silver such sable features as theirs.

A girl, Eustacia Vye, had secretly replaced the young man who was to have played the Turkish Knight.

'Ah, the mummers, the mummers!' cried several guests at once. 'Clear a space for the mummers.'

Hump-backed Father Christmas then made a complete entry, swinging his huge club, and in a general way clearing the stage for the actors proper, while he informed the company in smart verse that he was come, welcome or welcome not; concluding his speech with

> 'Make room, make room, my gallant boys,
>   And give us space to rhyme;
> We've come to show Saint George's play,
>   Upon this Christmas time.'

Eustacia entered and defeated the Valiant Soldier. He fell,

...coming down like a log upon the stone floor with force enough to dislocate his shoulder. Then, after more words from the Turkish Knight, rather too faintly delivered, and statements that he'd fight Saint George and all his crew, Saint George himself magnificently entered with the well-known flourish –

> 'Here come I, Saint George, the valiant man,
>   With naked sword and spear in hand,
> Who fought the dragon and brought him to the slaughter,
> And by this won fair Sabra, the King of Egypt's daughter;
>   What mortal man would dare to stand
>   Before me with my sword in hand?'

This was the lad who had first recognised Eustacia; and when she now, as the Turk, replied with suitable defiance, and at once began the combat, the young fellow took especial care to use his sword as gently as possible.

Imagine that you are a member of a mumming group. If you are a girl then, like Eustacia, you must be playing the part secretly, as girls were not normally allowed to take part. Describe your preparation, your costumes and your performance. Any quotations you may wish to include can be taken from the play above.

Pronouns

A *pronoun* is a word which takes the place of a noun. In *The Return of the Native*, Hardy might have written:

Hump-backed Father Christmas then made a complete entry, swinging his huge club, and in a general way clearing the stage for the actors proper, while Father Christmas informed the company in smart verse that Father Christmas was come, welcome or welcome not . . .

This sentence would have been clumsy and unnecessarily long. The meaning is still clear if the words 'Father Christmas' are twice replaced by the pronoun 'he'. Hardy wrote:

Hump-backed Father Christmas then made a complete entry, swinging his huge club, and in a general way clearing the stage for the actors proper, while he informed the company in smart verse that he was come, welcome or welcome not . . .

We usually replace nouns with pronouns (I, me, we, us, you, he, him, she, her, it, they and them) where their use does not make the meaning uncertain.

Exercise 2

Write out the following passage, replacing the words in *italics* with pronouns.

The carol-singers decided that *the carol-singers* should meet outside St Peter's Church. The weather was good that night and *the singers* were glad that *the weather* was not cold. As *the singers* could not remember the words of their carols, *the singers* had *the carols* printed on sheets. The leader of the singers carried a tin, and *the leader* asked people to put money in *the tin*. A man asked *the leader* if *the singers* intended to keep the money but *the leader* replied that a charity had given *the singers* permission to collect on behalf of *the charity*. An old lady told *the singers* that when *the old lady* had been young lots of money had been given to *the lady* for singing carols. A stray dog began to follow the singers, its head drooping as *the dog* walked behind *the singers*. At the end of their expedition *the singers* returned to the church hall for refreshments, not noticing the dog as *the dog* crouched in the shadows.

Exercise 3

Write out the following passage, underlining the pronouns which it contains.

The three children moved softly as they came down the stairs. Their mother slept on. She was unaware that they were already awake. They crept along the hall, eager to leave the shadows it contained. At the end of it they stopped, opened the sitting-room door and entered. Helen turned on the tree's lights. For a moment she shielded her eyes from the brightness.

Presents lay under the Christmas tree. In the shiny paper that covered them she saw the lights reflected. The children gazed at the presents, wanting to touch them. At last Helen stepped forward. She knelt a foot away from the nearest package. It was long and flat, and the paper covering it was green. She grasped its silver ribbon.

'Shall I open it?' she asked.

'We'll be in trouble if you do,' her sister answered.

Further reading

Many books have been written which deal with Christmas. You will probably enjoy the following novels and short stories:
The Thirteen Days of Christmas by Jenny Overton
The Giant under the Snow by John Gordon
The First Christmas Stocking by Reginald Nettel
Christmas in Wales by Dylan Thomas (from *Quite Early One Morning*)
The Wind in the Willows by Kenneth Grahame
I Want the Shiny Things by Stella Jones and *The Robin* by Barry Hines (both appear in an anthology called *Northern Drift*)

Plays about Christmas include:
Kidnapped at Christmas by Willis Hall
The Boy who wouldn't play Jesus by Bernard Kops
Folk Playtexts by Robert Leach (including some mummers' plays)

5 Waiting for the bell

Starting school

Starting a new school is always difficult. The experience may even be frightening. Most of you will remember starting school for the first time, when you were five. Since then you will have changed school at least once, and again faced the problem of becoming part of a new community, with its buildings, people and rules.

For discussion

- When you entered your present school, how did you feel?
- What had you heard about it before you joined? How far was what you had heard correct?
- Which aspects of the new school seemed frightening or confusing?
- How did you find your way around?
- What else might have been done to help you?

The following poem describes the thoughts of a small his or her first day at school.

First day at school

A millionbillionwillion miles from home
Waiting for the bell to go. (To go where?)
Why are they all so big, other children?
So noisy? So much at home they
must have been born in uniform
Lived all their lives in playgrounds
Spent the years inventing games
that don't let me in. Games
that are rough, that swallow you up.

And the railings.
All around, the railings.
Are they to keep out wolves and monsters?
Things that carry off and eat children?
Things you don't take sweets from?
Perhaps they're to stop us getting out
Running away from the lessins. Lessin.
What does a lessin look like?
Sounds small and slimy.
They keep them in glassrooms.
Whole rooms made out of glass. Imagine.

I wish I could remember my name
Mummy said it would come in useful.
Like wellies. When there's puddles.
Yellowwellies. I wish she was here.
I think my name is sewn on somewhere
Perhaps the teacher will read it for me,
Tea-cher. The one who makes the tea.

ROGER McGOUGH

Talking about the poem

1. Why does the school seem so far from home?
2. What does the child think of the other pupils?
3. How does the child feel on his or her first day?
4. What do the railings suggest to the child?

5   How has he or she misheard or misunderstood things about the school?
6   What has the child's mother done to help him or her cope with starting school?
7   How far does this poem remind you of your first day at primary school?

Writing an account

Write an account of your first day at your present school. That is likely to be a day you remember well, though by now it may seem far in the past.

Your account should have a beginning, a middle and an end. The beginning will probably be a description of your feelings before you left for school and your thoughts about what was going to happen. The middle will be a description of the various stages of the day in school – perhaps the assembly, division into forms, break, dinner, lessons and the end of the afternoon. The ending might be your thoughts at the end of the day.

You should put everything that you want to say about a particular part or event of the day into a single paragraph. Then, when you are going to deal with the next stage, begin a new paragraph by starting a new line and put the first word about an inch in from the margin. Then your reader knows that you have finished all you have to say on the first topic and that you are going on to talk about something else. Your account might be arranged in the following way:

Paragraph 1: Your thoughts at breakfast time.
Paragraph 2: The assembly for new pupils.
Paragraph 3: Being put into a form, a description of your form room and form tutor.
Paragraph 4: Break.
Paragraph 5: Your first lessons.
Paragraph 6: Dinner time.
Paragraph 7: Afternoon lessons.
Paragraph 8: The end of school for the afternoon.
Paragraph 9: Your thoughts at the end of the day.

If this is not the way your first day was spent, alter the arrangement to make it more suitable.

Three pieces of soap

The following passage describes part of Michael's first day in a new school. This was a country school, and very different from the town schools which Michael had attended before. In those he had met a wide variety of teachers, ranging from the young and gentle Miss Bar to the cruel Mr Tarlton. Now he had to weigh up a new set of teachers and a new headmaster, Mr Noake, who was investigating the disappearance of some soap.

A rather beautiful lady came through a door at the far end of the room at this moment, carrying a tray. She reminded me of Miss Bar. She gave tea to the three teachers and then to Mr Noake. He took a teacup, and drank from it quickly. Then he put it down and waited till the lady with the tray had gone through the door. On her way, I heard one of the teachers call her Mrs Noake. I couldn't believe it.

'*Soap*,' roared Noake, suddenly. 'That's where I was! Who took three pieces of soap? Three pieces of fresh yellow soap from the washbowl?'

There was a frightened silence. Yet somehow, from behind at least, I was coming to like Noake. He was a bully, but not a cruel one like Tarlton.

'I'll give you ten seconds. Sheila, was it you?'

A pretty girl, still flat-chested, blushed and said without breath, 'No – Mr Noake.'

'It was last time, you know.'

'Yes, Mr Noake.'

'And the time before that.'

'Yes, Mr Noake.'

'Not this time?'

'No, Mr Noake.'

'Go and look in your pocket, dear!'

Sheila got up, burning, and crept from the room. The class knew she was guilty. I knew, and I had only just arrived. We could tell, even if Noake could not. But he could.

Sheila came back in tears, surprised real tears, splashing tears, and burst out 'They're not there, Mr Noake. Honest, honest, honest.'

'I know,' said Noake. 'I am glad you are telling the truth to me. It is far worse to lie about stealing than it is just to steal. You did steal the soap, didn't you?'

'Yes, Mr Noake.'

'And now someone's stolen it from you. It's a shock, isn't it?'
'Yes, Mr Noake.'
'Go and help my wife wash up, there's a good girl. She needs some help.'

Gratefully, still crying she ran out of the room.

Perhaps, standing where I was I was the only person who saw Noake open his desk drawer and drop in three pieces of soap.

He turned to me. 'You'll be in Miss Rose's class. You'll be happy here. We're all happy. None of your sloppy town ways, mind!'

I sat down in front of the skinny woman and we started to borrow ten. It was all right.

MICHAEL BALDWIN   *Grandad with Snails*

Talking about the passage

1 Why did Mr Noake pause in his investigation until his wife had closed the door?
2 Why could Michael not believe that the lady was Mrs Noake?
3 How cruel was Mr Noake?
4 How did he try to teach Sheila a lesson?
5 'It is far worse to lie about stealing than it is just to steal.' Do you agree?

Writing about the passage

1 What did Michael think of Mrs Noake?
2 Why did Mr Noake ask Sheila if she had taken the soap?
3 What made her cry?
4 Why did Mr Noake send Sheila to help his wife wash up?
5 Michael felt that, 'It was all right.' Why?
6 Why would you like or not like to have Mr Noake as a teacher?
7 What qualities would you want a teacher to have?

Adjectives

An *adjective* is a word which describes a noun. Usually the adjective tells us to what kind of person or thing the writer or speaker is referring:

*The **old** school was surrounded by **green** fields.*
*The **excited little** boy rushed through the **open** door.*

Exercise 1

Rewrite the following sentences, underlining the adjectives which they contain.

1. Jill went to her new school on Tuesday.
2. It was a large building and stood at the end of a narrow road.
3. She waited at the main door with the rest of the new pupils.
4. They were led into a vast hall by an elderly teacher, where an unsmiling line of teachers was waiting.
5. To Jill the school seemed terrifying, and its noise deafening.
6. The elderly teacher read out a long list of names, which included that of Jill Thompson.
7. He told them that they would be in the form taken by Miss Phillips, a young lady on his left side.
8. She asked the children to follow her, and spoke with a quiet, pleasant voice.
9. They were led through long corridors, now silent but for the excited whispers of the new pupils.
10. They reached their form room, which had blue walls and was decorated with bright posters.

An adjective may tell us how many people or things there are: *The **two** classrooms each contained **several** children.*

Exercise 2

Rewrite the following sentences, underlining the adjectives which they contain.

1. The school had a thousand pupils and sixty teachers.
2. All pupils lived in the area around the school.
3. Some teachers lived in that area, but many teachers drove in every day from several other areas.
4. Six teachers lived in a town ten miles away from the school.
5. Jill was taught by twelve teachers and had to remember their twelve names and twelve personalities.
6. She had had only three teachers in her fourth year at the school she had left.
7. One teacher took her for most lessons, but for games and music she had other teachers.
8. The school she now attended, however, had many advantages.

9 It had, for example, six laboratories, three rooms for domestic science and four workshops.
10 For the first month she hated the school, for the second month she disliked it, but by the third month she was beginning to feel that she belonged there.

Other adjectives show the owner:
Her sons came home on **their** bicycles.

Exercise 3

Rewrite the following sentences, underlining the adjectives which they contain.

1 Jill told her mother little about her school.
2 When her mother asked questions, their effect was to make Jill say even less.

3   Her brother still went to the school which Jill had left and his comments on life there interested Jill.
4   She told him more about her school than she told their mother.
5   Its swimming pool fascinated him and its workshops also appealed to him.
6   He looked forward to when his chance to use its facilities would come.
7   He liked his school but it seemed that its work did not have the excitement of the work he knew Jill was now doing.
8   She was learning French and he had to hide his envy.
9   Their parents worried about both their children, about her silence and his boredom.
10 Their concern for Jill made them want to visit her new school as soon as possible.

Writing your own poem

Look at the picture of junior school children. Write a poem describing their thoughts, or your thoughts as you look at the picture.

The new boy

Jimmy Stewart had been sent to a secondary school for the first time. On his first morning at school he was put into the form taken by Mr Harris, who was very strict. The boys in the class told Jimmy that the teacher's name was Charlie Harris, and that there were two things that Jimmy must remember if he was to stay out of trouble with the teacher. The first was to pay his dinner money on time. Jimmy showed them the dinner money that his mother had given him.

Ginger beamed. 'You've got a clever mother, Stew. You give Charlie five bob and you'll be over the first danger. The other one's this. You don't ever call him "Charlie". Not to his face I mean. You call him "Charlie" and he'll bury you. You've got to call him "Charles". What school were you at last?'

'I've never been to school before,' I said.

They gaped at me and somebody said, 'Can you read?'

'Of course I can,' I said. 'My mother and father have been educating me.'

There was a snigger. A little boy on the front row said, 'I'd like to see my dad educating me! He can't do my homework sums now!'

Ginger Evans winked at somebody and then looked again at me, his voice all friendliness, his eyes brilliant with mischief.

'Thought you might have been used to calling teachers "sir",' he said. 'You don't do that with Charlie. He's one of these modern teachers. You call him "Charles" and you stick "Charles" on to everything you say if you don't want him to belt you. "Yes, Charles." That's how you do it. "Thanks very much, Charles." Got it? You do that and you'll be O.K. That right, you lot?'

They were nodding and grinning, and one or two of them were near to bursting.

'You must think everybody's as daft as you are, Evans,' the big boy said.

Ginger didn't hear him. He was too anxious to fill me with information. 'Charlie's got a stick, kid. Keeps it in that cupboard. Most of the teachers don't cane you but Charlie does and Timber Thompson sometimes. Gutsy Collins – he takes P.T. – he uses a slipper. But Charlie's the one to watch. If he uses his stick on you it feels like you've been guillotined. So you give him five bob for your dinners so's he can spend it on whisky at night and you call him "Charles" and you'll be O.K. That's how we do it. Isn't that right, you lot?'

There were frenzied nods and giggles which were strangled when Mr Harris walked into the room. He looked at me.

'You're the new boy. Stewart, is it?'

'Yes, Charles,' I said.

There was a network of tiny purple veins over his cheeks and these were suddenly lost in the redness that flushed into his face. His bottom lip was slightly trembling.

REGINALD MADDOCK   *The Dragon in the Garden*

Talking about the passage

1 Why did Ginger Evans tell Jimmy to call Mr Harris 'Charles'?
2 Why did Jimmy believe Ginger?
3 In what other ways are newcomers to a school tested?
4 Why are teachers given nicknames?

Writing about the passage

1 Why did the boys gape at Jimmy?
2 How did Jimmy learn to read?

3 Why were the boys afraid of Mr Harris?
4 How did their fear show when Mr Harris entered the room?
5 What seems to have been Mr Harris's feelings when Jimmy called him 'Charles'?
6 Describe the impression of Ginger which we are given in this passage.
7 If you had been in Mr Harris's place, what would you have done when Jimmy called you 'Charles'?
8 Explain the meanings of the following words as they are used in the passage:
brilliant, guillotined, frenzied.

Choosing powerful adjectives

We are often lazy when choosing adjectives. When we speak we tend to use only a few repetitive adjectives that tell the hearer little, such as 'nice', 'good' and 'awful'. When people talk they rarely choose powerful adjectives. In writing, however, you must take great care to select adjectives effectively. Vague adjectives, (like those mentioned above) should always be avoided. The one which is used most commonly is 'nice'. What might these two sentences below mean?

The town is nice.
She is nice.

Exercise 4

Rewrite the following sentences, replacing 'nice' with more precise adjectives.

1 I hope the weather will be nice on Sunday.
2 It was nice of him to give her a present.
3 The old couple lived in a nice house.
4 The mayoress was presented with a nice bouquet.
5 It was a nice book that you sent me.
6 The girl who answered the door had a nice face.
7 During our holiday we visited many nice places.
8 The people next door are nice neighbours.
9 His garden is nice as he spends hours working on it.
10 The film I saw last night had a nice ending.

Writing a description

Write a short clear introduction for new pupils telling them about your school. It should answer the following questions:

1 Where is the school?
2 How many pupils does it contain? How old are they?
3 What are the buildings and how are they arranged?
4 Does the school have any special facilities? Does it have a swimming pool or a sports hall, for example?
5 What are the school grounds like? Are there playing fields around it?
6 Are there any other questions that should be answered?

If your account is to be read easily, then the material that it includes should be grouped into sections. One section should answer each of the questions (or group of questions) that you set yourself. To help your reader, you should put all that you have to say on a section into a single paragraph. Each paragraph is then a single stage in the account. The reader knows that when he or she finishes reading one paragraph that you have said all that you have to say on that subject, and that you are now going on to deal with another step or stage in the account. Remember that you show that you are starting a new paragraph by beginning a new line and putting the first word about one inch in from the margin.

In your account, choose your adjectives with care, to give as accurate an impression of the school as possible.

Revision of punctuation

Rewrite the following sentences, putting in capital letters and punctuation marks wherever they are needed.

1 the teacher gave out the examination papers
2 would the questions deal with the topics he had revised
3 philip did not like geography or mr scott
4 the test was concerned with canada
5 he could mark quebec montreal and ottawa on the map
6 he had however forgotten where to find toronto
7 which were the most important provinces for growing wheat

8   philip chewed his pen scratched his head and tried to remember
9   had john finished already
10 mr scott told the pupils to stop writing put down their pens and pass their papers to the front

Vocabulary

Nouns from place-names

In unit 3 you were told that some nouns came from the names of people. Other nouns came from the names of places. The game 'rugby' is named after the school where it was first played. 'Champagne' is named after the French province where it is made. The fruit called 'damson' gained its name as it originally came from Damascus.

Try to find the origins of the following nouns:
badminton, bayonet, calico, canary, canter, jersey, port (wine), sardine, sherry, worsted.

Loan words

If you have recently begun to study a foreign language, you have probably found that the language contains certain words which we use in English. Words which we borrow from other languages are called 'loan words'. When we borrow an object or an idea from another country we often borrow its name too. If you are studying French, you may have met the word *café* which means both 'coffee' and 'a small restaurant where coffee is served'. When small restaurants like those in France were introduced into Britain, the name 'café' was borrowed. The drink served in them, however, had been introduced earlier, and the name for it, 'coffee', was borrowed from Arabic.

In order to see the variety of languages from which we borrow words, try to find the languages from which the following words were taken:
algebra, bazaar, garage, khaki, piano, sherbet, tattoo (design on the skin), tea, tomato, yacht.

Further reading

All My Men by Bernard Ashley
This novel tells the story of a boy who moves from London to a town in Kent. He has to establish himself, in school and out of it.

Autumn Term by Antonia Forest
Nicky and Lawrie, the Marlow twins, find difficulty in starting a new school already attended by four of their sisters, one of whom is Head Girl.

The Diddakoi by Rumer Godden
Kizzy, a half-gypsy, is persecuted by the pupils of a school to which she is sent, but she is determined to remain different from the other children.

Striker by Kenneth Cope
A new boy comes to an area with a poor football team, consisting of local schoolboys. He is not easily accepted by its members until they discover how skilful he is. The great problem, however, is his father, who has forbidden him to play.

6 Writing about the past

In the following extract from *Dawn Wind*, Rosemary Sutcliff is dealing with a lonely survivor on the field of a battle which took place one thousand five hundred years ago.

Authors frequently deal with experiences they have never had, and places and times which they have never known. Sometimes they even describe places and times that have never existed. They imagine their settings in great detail until they see, hear, smell and feel them.

The stories you will write best are probably those set in places you know well, describing events that you have experienced. Often, however, you will want to experiment with stories about things that have never happened to you, set in places and times that you have never known.

Even if you are not familiar with the subject and setting, it is wise to deal with people whom you understand. The characters should not be particular individuals whom you know, but they may show characteristics you have seen in friends and relatives. The great advantage of dealing with people whom you understand is that you can imagine with some confidence how the characters will act in the situations which you create.

The boy in the passage from *Dawn Wind* is a fugitive, a person running away from someone or something. His situation is real to us because Rosemary Sutcliff has imagined it so clearly that she could hear the moorhen's call and the wind blowing through the hawthorn bushes.

The survivor

The moon drifted clear of a long bank of cloud, and the cool slippery light hung for a moment on the crest of the high ground, and then spilled down the gentle bush-grown slope to the river. Between the darkness under the banks the water which had been leaden grey woke into moving ripple-patterns, and a crinkled skin of silver light marked where the paved ford carried across the road from Corinium to Aquae Sulis.* Somewhere among the matted

* Cirencester to Bath.

islands of rushes and water-crowfoot, a moorhen cucked and was still. On the high ground in the loop of the river nothing moved at all, save the little wind that ran shivering through the hawthorn bushes.

For a long while that was all, and then in the dark heart of the hawthorn tangle something rustled that was not the wind. It stirred, and was still, and then stirred again with a kind of whimpering gasp, dragging itself forward little by little out of the black shadows among the thorn roots, like a wounded animal. But it was no animal that crawled painfully into the moonlight at last, it was a boy. A boy of fourteen or so, with a smear of blood showing dark on his forehead, and the same darkness clotted round the edges of the jagged rent in his leather sleeve.

He propped himself on his left arm, his head hanging low between his shoulders; and then, as though with an intolerable effort, forced it upward and looked about him. Westward along the high ground the ring of ancient earthworks where the British had made their last night's camp stood mute and deserted now, empty of meaning as an unstrung harp, against the ragged sky. Far down the shallow valley, the camp-fires of the Saxons flowered red in the darkness, and between the dead camp and the living one, all along the river bank and over the high ground and along the line of the road to Aquae Sulis, stretched an appalling stillness scattered with the grotesque, twisted bodies of men and horses.

Only a few hours ago, all that stretch of stillness had been a thundering battle-ground, and on that battle-ground, the boy's world had died.

ROSEMARY SUTCLIFF *Dawn Wind*

Talking about the passage

1 How does Rosemary Sutcliff create atmosphere and suspense in the first two paragraphs?
2 How does she make the reader use his or her senses in these paragraphs?
3 What does the writer mean when she says '. . . on that battle-ground, the boy's world had died'?

Writing about the passage

Answer the following questions in complete sentences and, as far as possible, in your own words.

1 Describe the scene at night on the battlefield.
2 Why did the writer call the light 'cool' and 'slippery'?
3 What was the condition of the boy who emerged from the bushes?
4 Compare the two camps.
5 How successful is Rosemary Sutcliff in making the scene and the boy's situation real?
6 Describe the thoughts which you would expect the boy to have had.
7 Give a word or phrase which means the same as each of the following words as they are used in the passage:
intolerable, earthworks, appalling, grotesque.

Writing a story

Write a story called 'The fugitive'. Your account should make clear to your reader the feelings of the fugitive, which may be human or animal. Try to form a vivid picture in your mind of the setting, past or present, because then you can include the concrete details which will make your essay convincing. Take care to begin and end the essay effectively. It might be most successful to start when the fugitive's flight is already in progress, and to end when the fugitive is still fleeing.

Every story that you write should have a clear structure. It should have a beginning, a middle and an end. The middle should be divided into separate stages, and each of these stages dealt with in a single paragraph.

You might choose to deal with the story 'The fugitive' by writing about a girl who has run away from a workhouse in the nineteenth century. You would plan the stages of the story, giving a paragraph to each.

Paragraph 1: Girl wakes in barn – cold, hungry, frightened. She goes to seek food. Dogs bark, and wake farmer.
Paragraph 2: Girl chased by dogs but escapes down a stream. Seeks help at a cottage. Old woman takes her in.
Paragraph 3: Girl tells the woman her life story, especially life in workhouse and her escape. She mentions that there is a reward for her capture.
Paragraph 4: Girl sleeps. Woman leaves secretly. Girl recaptured, betrayed by the woman. The girl is placed in a cart.
Paragraph 5: Travelling through a stormy night, the captors taunt

Paragraph 6: the girl and threaten to punish her. Lightning scares the horses, which bolt. Cart overturns.
Girl escapes and runs into darkness, afraid but determined not to be trapped again.

You may use this plan for your story, or you may form a plan of your own.

Verbs

A *verb* is usually a word which tells us what someone or something did or is doing:
The moon **drifted** *clear of a long bank of cloud . . .*

Exercise 1

Rewrite the following passage, underlining the verbs which it contains.

When the warning came, the men rushed from their houses. Some clutched axes and others gripped swords. Those who owned no metal weapons carried heavy wooden clubs. A few wore ancient helmets. They gathered in the centre of the village and talked excitedly as they waited for their leader.
He arrived and began his speech. He told them that they faced great danger. Their enemies intended their destruction and had prepared an attack. He encouraged his people and praised their bravery. He then marched at their head to the ford which led to the village.

A few verbs do not describe an action, but show what someone or something is, seems or becomes:
He **is** *not afraid.*
The situation **seems** *to be hopeless.*
They **became** *certain of victory.*

Exercise 2

Rewrite the following sentences, underlining the verbs which they contain.

1 They were ready for battle at the ford.

2 During their wait the minutes seemed long.
3 Some men even became doubtful that their enemies were on the march.
4 The warning seemed far in the past.
5 The leader appeared calm and confident.
6 As they were half-certain of their safety they became aware of a distant sound.
7 The noise became louder and the day seemed colder.
8 Their fear was greater as their enemies were near.
9 Their weapons seemed heavier and less effective.
10 The battle was close and all were at prayer.

Choosing verbs

It is particularly important that verbs are chosen carefully. Some writers, who use adjectives very skilfully, spoil their work by using verbs that have little force. Well-chosen verbs make a passage powerful:

The dog stopped. There was complete silence and then, like a cruel wind *creaking* the door of an abandoned house, came a laugh. It *gibbered* in the hall, finding its way through cracks in the air to *rake* their hair with bony fingers and *tug* at their scalps.

Exercise 3

In the following sentences the verbs are not very interesting. Rewrite the sentences, replacing the words in *italic* with more precise alternatives.

1 When the girl *got* her prize she *went* to tell her parents.
2 The frightened horse *went* down the road.
3 A graceful swan *went* across the lake.
4 The apprentice only *got* a small weekly wage.
5 The man *got up* when he smelled the smoke and *got* the fire brigade.
6 The lady *got* into her car and *went* down the road.
7 As the birds *got* their food, a cat *went* towards them.
8 The thief *went* down the road and the crowd *went* after him.
9 The seawall broke and water *went* into the village.
10 She *got* angrier when they *got* home.

Treasure!

If you discovered a hoard of treasure, what would your reaction be? Treasure is sometimes found by accident but often it is discovered by people who have dedicated much of their lives to a search for it. One of the most exciting discoveries of this century was the treasure in the Saxon burial ship at Sutton Hoo.

In the Old English poem *Beowulf*, there is a burial mound containing treasure, guarded by a dragon. Beowulf kills the dragon, but is fatally wounded by it. After Beowulf's death, a burial mound is made for him, filled with the treasure he has won.

> In the mound they rested   rings and jewels
> and all the battle-gear   buried in the hoard,
> taken thence by men   dreaming of war.
> They let the earth hold   the treasure of earls,
> gold in the dust   where it yet lies
> as useless to men   as it was of old.
>   MARGARET WILLIAMS   *Wordhoard*

In the poem which follows, discuss how the hoard affects those who come into contact with it and what you think the poet is trying to suggest about treasure. Then answer the questions that follow the poem.

The hoard

> When the moon was new and the sun young
> of silver and gold the gods sung:
> in the green grass they silver spilled,
> and the white waters they with gold filled.
> Ere the pit was dug or Hell yawned,
> ere dwarf was bred or dragon spawned,
> there were Elves of old, and strong spells
> under green hills in hollow dells
> they sang as they wrought many fair things,
> and the bright crowns of the Elf-kings.
> But their doom fell, and their song waned,
> by iron hewn and by steel chained.
> Greed that sang not, nor with mouth smiled,
> in dark holes their wealth piled,
> graven silver and carven gold:
> over Elvenhome the shadow rolled.

There was an old dwarf in a dark cave,
to silver and gold his fingers clave;
with hammer and tongs and anvil-stone
he worked his hands to the hard bone,
and coins he made, and strings of rings,
and thought to buy the power of kings.
But his eyes grew dim and his ears dull
and the skin yellow on his old skull;
through his bony claw with a pale sheen
the stony jewels slipped unseen.
No feet he heard, though the earth quaked,
when the young dragon his thirst slaked,
and the stream smoked at his dark door.
The flames hissed on the dank floor,
and he died alone in the red fire;
his bones were ashes in the hot mire.

There was an old dragon under grey stone;
his red eyes blinked as he lay alone.
His joy was dead and his youth spent,
he was knobbed and wrinkled, and his limbs bent
in the long years to his gold chained;
in his heart's furnace the fire waned.
To his belly's slime gems stuck thick,
silver and gold he would snuff and lick:
he knew the place of the least ring
beneath the shadow of his black wing.
Of thieves he thought on his hard bed,
and dreamed that on their flesh he fed,
their bones crushed, and their blood drank:
his ears drooped and his breath sank.
Mail-rings rang. He heard them not.
A voice echoed in his deep grot:
a young warrior with a bright sword
called him forth to defend his hoard.
His teeth were knives, and of horn his hide,
but iron tore him, and his flame died.

There was an old king on a high throne:
his white beard lay on knees of bone;
his mouth savoured neither meat nor drink,
nor his ears song; he could only think
of his huge chest with carven lid

where pale gems and gold lay hid
in secret treasury in the dark ground;
its strong doors were iron-bound.
The swords of his thanes were dull with rust,
his glory fallen, his rule unjust,
his halls hollow, and his bowers cold,
but king he was of elvish gold.
He heard not the horns in the mountain-pass,
he smelt not the blood on the trodden grass,
but his halls were burned, his kingdom lost;
in a cold pit his bones were tossed.

There is an old hoard in a dark rock,
forgotten behind doors none can unlock;
that grim gate no man can pass.
On the mound grows the green grass;
there sheep feed and the larks soar,
and the wind blows from the sea-shore.
The old hoard the Night shall keep,
while earth waits and the Elves sleep.

J R R TOLKIEN

Talking about the poem

1 Who created the hoard and how were they destroyed?
2 Why did the old dwarf work the precious stones and gold?
3 Describe the attitude of the dragon towards the hoard.
4 What effect did the treasure have upon the king?
5 Does this poem teach you anything about the power of riches? Give reasons for your answer.
6 Do you think money can buy happiness? Again give reasons for your answer.

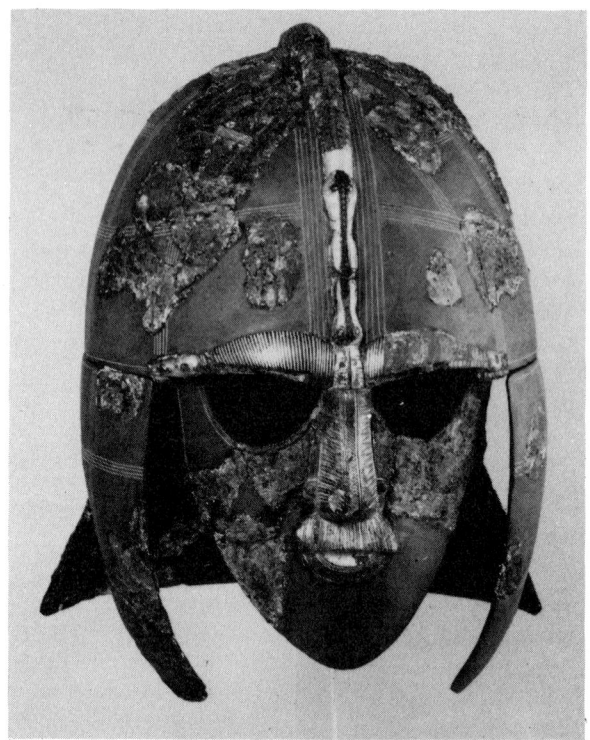

Writing your own poem

Imagine that you find a hoard of treasure or weapons, or a single object from the Saxon period. Write a poem about it, describing your feelings on finding it, and the thoughts that it suggests to you.

Apostrophes

When you are writing speech, or a letter to a friend, you may use shortened forms such as 'didn't' and 'couldn't' instead of using 'did not' and 'could not'. When you shorten any word, an *apostrophe* is used to mark the place of the missing letter or letters.

If, for example, 'was not' is shortened to 'wasn't', an apostrophe is used to show that the 'o' of 'not' has been missed out.

If 'it is' is shortened to 'it's', then an apostrophe is used to show that the 'i' of 'is' has been missed out.

Exercise 4

Rewrite the following passage, using apostrophes wherever they are needed.

Olaf sat amongst his men who talked quietly about the coming raid.
'The men dont know why we should risk a daylight landing,' whispered Thor to his chief.
'I shouldnt worry,' replied Olaf, 'I wont let you down. Im familiar with this coast. No one will see us land.'
'Thats all very well, but the men are still worried,' insisted Thor. 'Theres too much at risk as it is.'
'Thats why its worth it. I wouldnt risk all our lives if I wasnt sure.'
'Thats as may be,' grumbled Thor, 'but if we dont get killed on land this leaking hulk wont get us back through that sea.'
'If you or they dont like it,' growled Olaf, 'then you shouldnt have come. Come on, lets get some sleep. We shall need as much rest as we can get.'

Fur and fang

While a boy and girl are on a journey, across the countryside on foot and at night, they are chased by wolves. Elfwyn, the boy, sees the creatures in the moonlight. The children try to find shelter in a ruined Roman building in a wood, which is surrounded by statues and which seems to be deserted.

The leaders of the pack were now in view. Fangs and eyes flashed as they came swerving through the jumble of scrub and ruin. Halfway up the staircase Elfwyn turned at the foot of one massive, helmeted figure – even in that wild moment of panic his eyes could not help reading, half-consciously the letters graven on the pedestal. AJAX the inscription ran.
'Get up!' he panted.
'What about –'
'Get up!' He clapped a hand to the seat of her breeches and heaved her up.
'All right – I'll manage! Look out for yourself, Elfwyn!'
As he turned and sprang towards the next of the giant figures, he saw that he had left it too late. The first wolf was at the foot of the staircase and would spring on his shoulders before he could climb

beyond reach. He faced it with levelled spear. The snarling grey shadow seemed to gather itself together and then rose in the air.

Judith screamed. And then, as it seemed, a miracle happened. She heard no new sound amid the general confusion, but she saw the wolf turn a grotesque sort of somersault, as though an invisible hand had reached out and struck it in the midst of its spring. It crashed clumsily down upon the time-worn steps, well below where Elfwyn was standing, and went rolling and writhing to the bottom. There, after a few moments, it gave a final twitch and lay still.

The boy was so astounded that he could only stare down at it. The spear in his hand was still bloodless, he had felt no shock, he knew that the wolf had never even brushed the point.

'Now's your chance!' Judith besought him urgently. 'Quick – before the others –'

But again he had left it too late. There were other wolves close at the heels of the first. Four of them came up the stairs abreast, a surging wave of fur and fang. Elfwyn gave himself up for lost. Whether he stood his ground or turned his back they would overwhelm him and drag him down. So he faced them, legs braced, protected from behind by one of the great pedestals. And the wolves came on . . .

It was as though someone had heaved a sigh – as though a whisper had passed through the moonbeams slanting down upon the stairway. One of the wolves yelped, gurgled, and fell back. An arrow stuck out of its throat, making a pale straight wand of light.

GEOFFREY TREASE   *Mist over Athelney*

Talking about the passage

1 What qualities does Elfwyn show in this passage?
2 How does the writer make the wolves seem frightening?
3 How does the author make this passage exciting?

Writing about the passage

Answer the following questions in complete sentences and, as far as possible, in your own words.

1 How did the children try to escape from the wolves at the beginning of the passage?
2 Why did Elfwyn have to face the first wolf?
3 What was the 'miracle'?
4 Why did Elfwyn know that he had not killed the first wolf?
5 How did he feel as he faced the rest of the wolves?
6 Describe the events of the passage as if you were Judith.
7 Give a word or phrase which means the same as each of the following words, as used in the passage:
graven, pedestal, writhing, wand.

Riddles

The Anglo-Saxons produced much fine poetry that still exists but what remains can only be a tiny proportion of what was written. They enjoyed riddles. The following Anglo-Saxon riddles have been translated into modern English. Try to work out the answers to them.

1   Silent is my dress when I step across the earth,
    Reside in my house, or ruffle the waters.
    Sometimes my adornments and this high windy air
    Lift me over the livings of men,
    The power of the clouds carries me far
    Over all people. My white pinions
    Resound very loudly, ring with a melody,
    Sing out clearly, when I sleep not on
    The soil or settle on grey waters . . . a travelling spirit.

2   On earth there's a warrior of curious origin.
    He's created, gleaming, by two dumb creatures
    For the benefit of men. Foe bears him against foe
    To inflict harm. Women often fetter him,
    Strong as he is. If maidens and men
    Care for him with due consideration
    And feed him frequently, he'll faithfully obey them
    And serve them well. Men succour him for the warmth
    He offers in return; but this warrior will cruelly punish
    Anyone who permits him to become too proud.
                    BRUCE MITCHELL (ED)   *The Battle of Maldon
                                          and other Old English Poems*

(Answers on page x)

Writing your own poem

Write a riddle of your own. Choose an object or an animal and, without naming it, describe its appearance and behaviour as vividly as you can so that your readers may guess what it is.

Fire!

A Viking raid is taking place. English men, women and children have sheltered inside a church, the door of which they have barricaded. An archbishop is celebrating Mass when shouts are heard outside.

Someone cried out, 'Fire! They are bringing fire!' And indeed, through the darkened chinks in the door faint wisps of smoke were drifting, curling. Screaming horribly the crowd stampeded to the far end of the church. They overran the precinct of the altar, and the archbishop, who till now had stood alone, was lost among them. The kindling that had been piled up outside leapt into flame, with a great roar like the sound of a river in spate. Smoke diffused in the air along the nave; high up the pale cool walls of stone it wound, snake-like, along the intricate linked arches carved there, and floated upwards to the painted angels on the roof. The stench of burning smarted in the back of men's throats. They coughed. Their eyes ran.

Suddenly a fierce light glowed upon the walls; the lattice in the window was a sheet of flame. A great tongue of fire was sucked inwards through it, and upwards towards the roof. Sparks blew in, and black cinders fell over the heads of the people. In only a few seconds the roof beams were alight. A great wave of fire swept along the church roofing it all with flame. There was no way out, for all the doors were barricaded. By now the fire had eaten through the timbers of the west door, but the great beams that had framed the door still stood, like the bars of hell itself, a black grid against a blinding sheet of flame. Then, with a noise like a clap of thunder, the west wall cracked in the heat, and a tumble of coping-stones fell from the doorway-arch.

It was a monk who ran first. He ran straight into the fire, flinging himself upon the blazing framework of the door, shrieking as he went. The charred beams were nearly eaten away; the trellis of burning wood collapsed as he charged through. Then there was a gap in the fire; one could see through to the open air. It was a way too terrible for most; but after a few moments another monk scrambled over the piles of glowing charcoal, and went running, with the hem of his robe on fire, on to the points of a bank of spears levelled to meet him beyond. Only when the roof began to fall in did the great crowd rush to follow him.

JILL PATON WALSH   *Thurkell the Tall*

Talking about the passage

1   Why did the English take refuge in a church during the Viking raid?
2   Can you explain the actions of the two monks?
3   How does the writer make her description of the fire vivid?

Writing about the passage

Answer the following questions in complete sentences and, as far as possible, in your own words.

1 What were the earliest signs that the Vikings had set fire to the church?
2 How did the crowd first show its panic?
3 Describe how the fire spread.
4 What would be the feelings of the people in the church as they saw it burning?
5 Why was the doorway frightening?
6 What would happen as the people left the church?
7 Give a word or phrase which means the same as each of the following as they are used in the passage:
precinct, spate, diffused, intricate.

Writing a story

Study the extract below from *The Horned Helmet* by Henry Treece, which describes a raid from the attackers' point of view. What makes this narrative exciting?

At last, when torches flared out from the fishing-boats among the herring shoals, and men's loud voices came up the cliff as the laden nets were drawn in, Jarl Skallagrim passed the word round that the time had come. The men tied strips of sheepskin round their feet and set off in a long line, up among the gorse and the tussocky grass.

Beorn's heart thumped so hard, he thought everyone would hear, but no one mentioned it. No one spoke at all. The whole shipload of men moved like ghosts in the dark, silently. Only when they stood on a mound, an arrow's flight from the lighted village, did Thorgaut whisper, 'Stay between Odd and me, my boy. Do not go off on your own.' He had no need to say this, for now Beorn was far too frightened to leave them.

There was no stockade round the cluster of stone huts, for this was a village of fishermen, not herdsmen. The highest building was a wooden hall of black oak, with a steep thatched roof.

Odd pointed with his axe and whispered, 'Their chief's house. There the treasure will be. There Starkad and Skallagrim will be found at the fighting's sunset.'

Beorn's legs were trembling as though he had run a mile. His fingers lost their use and he dropped his cudgel in the darkness and did not even bother to search for it. He was so afraid. But, when the battle-run started, he forgot his fear and dashed in and out of the houses yelling like everyone else – though he hardly knew what he was yelling about.

In the extract, the raid is being described by someone who is not himself taking part in the story. This kind of writing, in which the pronouns used are 'he', 'she', 'it' and 'they', is said to be *in the third person*. Some writers prefer to write as if the story is being told by one of the characters taking part:

I woke abruptly and sat up in the icy greyness of the January dawn. What is that noise? Again . . . Who is blowing trumpets at this hour of the morning? I heard shouting. Heavy footsteps clattered over the paving stones below. I could hear the chink of mail; the rattle of a dropped shield, sliding and bumping down the stairs. Then once more that strident, heart-quickening bay of trumpets!

Such writing, where the pronouns 'I' and 'we' are often used, is said to be *in the first person*. If an author has one of his characters tell, or narrate, the story, that character is called *the narrator*.

It is important that, when you decide whether to tell your story in the first person or the third person, you make sure that you do not forget your decision while writing the story. An accidental change, such as that in the paragraph below, confuses the reader.

As I glanced about me I saw that the chest had disappeared. He kicked the rubbish left in the corner and there, hastily-hidden, was the chest. I saw that the coffer-lid had been split across.

Imagine that you are either a raider or a victim of a raid. Write an account of the raid in the first person. It does not have to be a Viking raid. It could be set in the present day or in any historical period. Form a clear picture in your mind of the setting and of the other people involved. Your story should have a most exciting stage, a most memorable incident, which is called the *climax*. This should come quite close to the end of the story. If the climax is too early in the story the incidents that follow it may not seem very interesting and your reader will become bored. You should lead up to the most memorable incident, and the reader should be kept in suspense for as long as possible, waiting to know what is going to happen.

If you choose to write about a Viking raid, you might use the following plan:

Paragraph 1: A description of your peaceful Saxon village, near the sea.

Paragraph 2: You leave your family and begin a journey on foot.
Paragraph 3: Stopping to rest, you see smoke rising behind you, and realise that a building in your village is burning. You hurry towards it.
Paragraph 4: The climax – from a distance, too far away to help, you see the later stages of the raid.
Paragraph 5: You return to your destroyed village, where no living people are left. A description of your feelings.

Vocabulary

Modern English developed from the language of the Anglo-Saxons but many English words were borrowed from Latin and Greek. Sometimes you can guess the meaning of a word by thinking about the Latin or Greek word on which it is based. The basis of a word is called its *root*.

For instance, the Latin word *manus*, meaning 'hand', provides the root of each of the following words: *manu*cure, *manu*al, *manu*script.

We use numerous words based on the Latin *scribo* and the Greek *grapho*, both of which mean 'I write'.

1 What are the meanings of the following words?
   a circumscribe, describe, inscription, manuscript, prescribe, scribble, scribe, script, scripture, transcript.
   b autograph, biography, geography, graph, graphic, graphite, graphology, heliograph, monograph, telegraph.
2 How many words can you find that are derived from the Latin *dictare*, meaning 'to say', and the Greek *skopeein*, meaning 'to look at'? (Look for words containing the syllables *dict* and *scope*.)

Further reading

Several authors have written novels which have Viking or Saxon settings. Some are listed below.

Henry Treece wrote many historical novels set between the Roman invasion of Britain and the Norman Conquest but he was primarily interested in the Viking period. In *Viking's Dawn, The Road to Miklagard* and *Viking's Sunset* he traces the life of Harald Sigurdson who sailed with the Vikings to search for treasure, facing icy seas and incredible hardships, and meeting bloodthirsty resistance.

Other novels by Henry Treece about this period are *The Last of the Vikings, Man with a Sword* and *Vinland the Good.*

Rosemary Sutcliff's books include:

Blood Feud
Jestyn, an English slave, becomes his Viking master's blood brother in the deadly feud to avenge Thormod's dead father.

Dawn Wind
Owain, a young Briton, slave of the Saxons, gains his freedom through faithful and courageous service.

Jill Paton Walsh has written:

Hengest's Tale
A haunting tragic tale of Finn, a legendary prince, and the feud between Danes, Jutes and Frisians during the Dark Ages.

With Kevin Crossley-Holland she has also written:

Wordhoard
A book of short stories about the Anglo-Saxons.

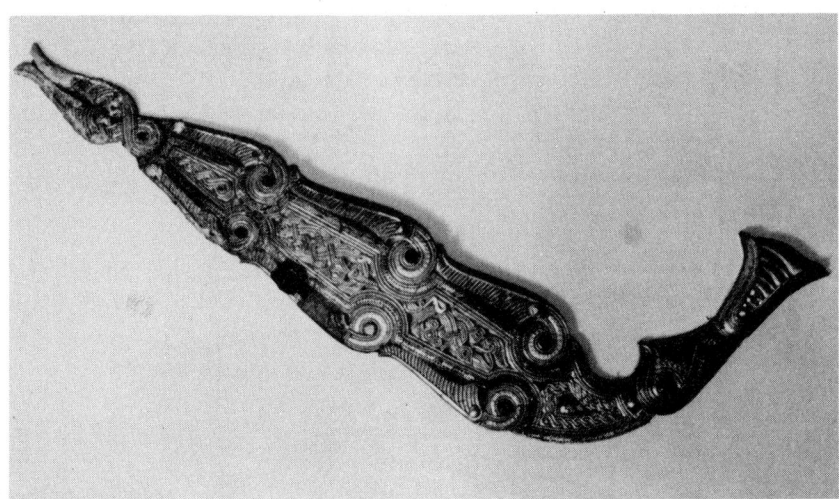

7 The moon and back

Writing about the future

In some ways, you have more freedom when you write about the past than when you write about the present. Everyone thinks that he or she knows what life today is like, but fewer readers have firm opinions about what happened at various times in the past. You have the greatest freedom, however, when writing about the future.

Although we know more and more about space and other planets, the universe still provides writers with unlimited possibilities. You can create your own world and your own forms of life. Remember, though, that no matter how strange your setting is, and how extraordinary the events that happen in it, you should always deal with people whom you know and understand.

Once writers who wrote about the moon had to guess what it was like:

Space travellers

There was a witch, hump-backed and hooded,
Lived by herself in a burnt-out tree.
When storm winds shrieked and the moon was buried
And the dark of the forest was black as black,
She rose in the air like a rocket at sea,
   Riding the wind,
   Riding the night,
Riding the tempest to the moon and back.

There may be a man with a hump of silver,
Telescope eyes and a telephone ear,
Dials to twist and knobs to twiddle,
Waiting for a night when the skies are clear,
To shoot from the scaffold with a blazing track,
   Riding the dark,
   Riding the cold,
Riding the silence to the moon and back.

JAMES NIMMO

Talking about the poem

1. How did the witch reach the moon?
2. What was the man mentioned in the second half of the poem?
3. What was the scaffold?
4. How was the witch's journey different from the man's?
5. Why do you think the poet chose to compare these two space travellers?

Writing your own poem

Imagine that you were the first person to be sent into space. After the tension of waiting and the pressure of blast-off, you are now higher than birds have ever flown, hurtling faster than any other person has ever travelled.

In orbit, you look out of your small window. Describe what you see, and your feelings.

Moon landing

We know now what the surface of the moon is like. It has been photographed, men have stood on it, and samples of rock and dust have been brought back to earth.

This is an edited extract from the recording of the first landing on the moon, made by Neil Armstrong and Buzz Aldrin, on 21st July, 1969.

ARMSTRONG:	Okay. I just checked – getting back to that first step, Buzz. It's not even collapsed too far but it's adequate to get back up. It takes a pretty good little jump. I'm at the foot of the ladder. The L.M. (Lunar Module) footpads are only depressed in the surface about one or two inches. Although the surface appears to be very finely grained as you get close to it, it's almost like a powder. Now and then it's very fine. I'm going to step off the L.M. now. That's one small step for man, one giant leap for mankind. As the surface is fine and powdery, I can pick it up loosely with my toe. It does adhere in fine layers like powdered charcoal to the sole and sides of my boots and the treads in fine sandy particles. There seems to be no difficulty in moving around as we suspected. It's perhaps even easier than the simulations that we performed on the ground. We're essentially on a level place here. I can see evidence of rays emanating from the descent engine, but a very insignificant amount. Okay Buzz, we're ready to bring down the camera . . . Looking up at Buzz in the shadow and I can see everything quite clearly. The light is sufficiently bright, backlighted into the front of the L.M. so that everything is very clearly visible.
ALDRIN:	Okay.
BASE:	You are doing well. Data is good.
ARMSTRONG:	I'll step out and take some of my first pictures here . . .
ALDRIN:	That looks beautiful from here, Neil.
ARMSTRONG:	It has a stark beauty all its own. It's like much of the high desert of the United States. It's different but it's very pretty out here . . .

Lunar journey

In the same year that Neil Armstrong stepped onto the surface of the moon John Christopher published The Lotus Caves. *It is set in the future, when men have lived in a colony on the moon for fifty years. Two boys, Marty and Steve, were bored with life in the Bubble, which housed the colony. They decided to explore the moon for themselves. They stole a tracked vehicle, called 'a crawler', though they knew they would be in trouble with the authorities.*

For the most part they saw only the walls of the valley or ravine through which the crawler was travelling, but occasionally there were glimpses of the high dazzling peaks of the mountains and once, from an eminence, a view of the Sea of Rains behind them, though not of the Bubble. They made one error by taking a wrong path into a cul-de-sac which stopped them dead after twenty minutes. Marty was at the wheel, Steve navigating. The crawler faced a wall of rock in which, Steve pointed out, there were gleaming flecks of something that was not ordinary stone.

'Gold?' Marty asked.

'False-gold, more likely. But it might be worth making a note of it.'

If they were able to report an important new site for mining, Marty thought, the authorities might go a little easier on them. The crawler backed up to the point which he recognized as the one where they had gone wrong, and he stopped fooling himself. Nothing was going to get them out of trouble when they went back to the Bubble. The best thing to do was not dwell on it.

They had crossed the spine of the foothills and were descending by the time Steve went into the bunk again. The descent was not a steady one, of course – there were twists and back-trackings and occasional quite steep climbs – but on the whole they were heading downwards and he was using the spikes from time to time to prevent a slide. Marty did not find the loneliness quite so overpowering this time, and the shift went reasonably quickly. At the end of six hours Steve reappeared and Marty took his place. He was very tired again and dropped off right away. The alarm woke him, and he came out to find the crawler heading along a dark and narrow canyon that dropped steeply in front of them. The walls were so close overhead that it was almost like being in a tunnel, and Steve had the headlights on to see his way.

It was tricky terrain, as Marty discovered when he took over. Both lights and grip-spikes had to be used frequently, and however much care one took it was impossible to prevent the crawler's treads occasionally losing adhesion and the crawler itself suddenly sliding, throwing the pair of them against one or another of the padded interior surfaces.

JOHN CHRISTOPHER   *The Lotus Caves*

Talking about the passage

1 What impression does John Christopher give of the moon's surface?
2 What do we learn about the crawler?
3 What made the journey difficult?

Writing about the passage

1 What could the boys see for most of the time?
2 Explain how the boys made a mistake.
3 Why did the boys make a note of the place where they saw the shining flecks?
4 What made the descent difficult?
5 How did Marty try to prevent the crawler from slipping?
6 Why did Steve have to put the headlights on?
7 Give the meanings of the following words as they are used in the passage:
   ravine, eminence, cul-de-sac, navigating, terrain, adhesion.
8 Explain how you would have felt if you had been in Marty's place.

Verbs

The extract from the recording of the astronauts talking is mainly in the *present tense*. That is to say, it sounds as if the actions are taking place at this moment:
It takes a pretty good little jump. I'm at the foot of the ladder.

The extract from *The Lotus Caves* is in the *past tense*. It sounds as if the actions took place at some time in the past:
At the end of six hours Steve reappeared and Marty took his place.

Exercise 1

Rewrite these sentences in the past tense.

1   The Bubble is a huge transparent dome, and contains a lake.
2   People travel across it in autocabins, which run on overhead cables.
3   The Moon people mine metals and send them back to the Earth.
4   They breed animals in factory farms, and grow fish in tanks.
5   They live in a world that has no seasons, where the daylight lasts for two weeks at a time.

Exercise 2

Rewrite these sentences in the present tense.

1   In the museum were many relics of the past.
2   The children liked seeing a model of a house which showed an ancient central-heating system.
3   A collection of primitive weapons included a gun which fired bullets.
4   An exhibition of twentieth-century clothes amused the children.
5   Mrs Green tried to explain why their ancestors' dress seemed so ugly and uncomfortable.

There are other tenses, which may consist of more than one word:
I have seen
I will have seen
I should have seen
I was seeing
Sometimes the words forming a verb may be separated:
I have not seen. I have just seen.

Exercise 3

Rewrite the following sentences, underlining all the words which make up the verbs.

1   The two boys had driven their crawler up a slope in the foothills.
2   They had reached the top of a hill.
3   They had never ventured so far before.
4   The highest of the planet's mountains was towering above them.
5   The crawler had frequently slipped on the loose stones.

6 They should have started for home earlier.
7 The long drive back was still awaiting them.
8 They had been resting in turns, but they had only slept a little.
9 The crawler had been turned and they were preparing their route for the return journey.
10 Mark had been looking towards the colony, but he had not yet realised that a glow was spreading in the sky above it.

Writing a story

You probably noticed how careful and observant Neil Armstrong was when he first set foot on the surface of the moon. Are these attitudes to be expected when someone encounters a new experience?

Imagine that you are a member of the crew of a spaceship which is sent to explore a planet no man has visited before. Who are your companions? What are they like? You orbit the planet, examining it from a distance, before landing. What kind of surface does it have? How and where do you land? Is the planet inhabited? If so, what lives there? The clearer your picture of the planet, and the more detail in which you imagine it, the more effective any reader will find your story. A possible plan for your story could be:

Paragraph 1: Approaching the planet.
Paragraph 2: The view from your orbit.
Paragraph 3: Landing, and your first close impression of the planet's surface.
Paragraph 4: You begin to explore the planet, and find a strange building.
Paragraph 5: It is deserted, but you find signs of its former inhabitants.
Paragraph 6: You return to your spacecraft. What do you find? What happens?

Apostrophes

Another use of the apostrophe is to show where one thing or person belongs to another:
the chief's spaceship.

The rules for the use of apostrophes to show possession are simple.
If the word standing for the owner or owners is singular, you add *'s*.
*The ring belonging to the **man** is called 'the **man's** ring'.*
*The uniform belonging to the **army** is called 'the **army's** uniform'.*

If the word standing for the owners is plural and does not end in 's', then you add *'s*.
*The craft belonging to the **men** is called 'the **men's** craft'.*

If the word standing for the owners is plural and ends in 's', then an apostrophe is added after the 's'.
*The weapons of the **warriors** are called 'the **warriors'** weapons'.*

Where would apostrophes be placed in the following expressions?
the spaceships door
the childrens games
the ladys jewels
the ladies jewels

Exercise 4

Rewrite the sentences below, replacing the phrase in *italics* with one which means the same but includes an apostrophe. For example,
The inhabitants of the planet *were friendly.*
would become
The planet's inhabitants *were friendly.*

1. *The craft of the explorers* came close to destruction on landing.
2. *The roughness of the surface* made it difficult to walk on.
3. At first there was no sign of *the creatures of the planet*.
4. Suddenly *the sides of the spaceship* were swarming with strange creatures.
5. *The leader of the creatures* gave a signal.
6. *The position of the earthmen* seemed desperate.
7. They were captured and taken to *the city of the creatures*.
8. *The buildings of the city* had high towers.
9. *The eyes of the prisoners* came to rest on a palace.
10. *The doors of the palace* opened, and the men were forced in.

Vocabulary

A *suffix* is a part of a word which is added after the root to change its meaning. The suffixes *-ful* and *-ous* are both used to form adjectives. The meaning of *-ful* is 'full of', a meaning which is often shared by *-ous*.

1. Explain the meanings of the following words, then use each in a sentence:
   a artful, beautiful, bountiful, deceitful, disdainful, graceful, plentiful, resentful, thoughtful, watchful.
   b courageous, courteous, dangerous, ferocious, furious, gracious, humorous, industrious, laborious, luminous.

The following poem may seem strange to you. It is not written in sentences, but poetry does not have to be. At first it may appear to be an unconnected series of phrases, each including one noun and one adjective. On closer examination, however, you will find that the poem tells a story. Try to work out what the story is, and how the poet manages to tell it.

Off course

    the golden flood   the weightless seat
    the cabin song   the pitch black
    the growing beard   the floating crumb
    the shining rendezvous   the orbit wisecrack
    the hot spacesuit   the smuggled mouth-organ
    the imaginary somersault   the visionary sunrise
    the turning continents   the space debris
    the golden lifeline   the space walk
    the crawling deltas   the camera moon
    the pitch velvet   the rough sleep
    the crackling headphone   the space silence
    the turning earth   the lifeline continents
    the cabin sunrise   the hot flood
    the shining spacesuit   the growing moon
      the crackling somersault   the smuggled orbit
      the rough moon   the visionary rendezvous
      the weightless headphone   the cabin debris
      the floating lifeline   the pitch sleep
      the crawling camera   the turning silence
      the space crumb   the crackling beard
      the orbit mouth-organ   the floating song

                                        EDWIN MORGAN

Writing your own poem

In *The Lotus Caves* John Christopher invented a plant which no man has ever seen. Other writers have invented creatures. Imagine either a plant or a creature that lives on another planet, which has never been seen by any human. When you have a clear picture of the plant or creature in your mind, give it a name, then write a poem describing it. When you have finished your rough draft read it through, asking yourself whether your reader will be able to imagine your creation. After you have made any necessary improvements, copy out your final version.

The fun they had

Margie even wrote about it that night in her diary. On the page headed 17 May, 2155, she wrote, 'Today Tommy found a real book!'

It was a very old book. Margie's grandfather once said that when he was a little boy *his* grandfather told him that there was a time when all stories were printed on paper.

They turned the pages, which were yellow and crinkly, and it was awfully funny to read words that stood still instead of moving the way they were supposed to – on a screen, you know. And then, when they turned back to the page before, it had the same words on it that it had had when they read it the first time.

'Gee,' said Tommy, 'what a waste. When you're through with the book, you just throw it away, I guess. Our television screen must have had a million books on it and it's good for plenty more. I wouldn't throw *it* away.'

'Same with mine,' said Margie. She was eleven and hadn't seen as many telebooks as Tommy had. He was thirteen.

She said, 'Where did you find it?'

'In my house.' He pointed without looking, because he was busy reading. 'In the attic.'

'What's it about?'

'School.'

Margie was scornful. 'School? What's there to write about school? I hate school.'

Margie always hated school, but now she hated it more than ever. The mechanical teacher had been giving her test after test in geography and she had been doing worse and worse until her mother had shaken her head sorrowfully and sent for the County Inspector.

He was a round little man with a red face and a whole box of tools with dials and wires. He smiled at Margie and gave her an apple, then took the teacher apart. Margie had hoped he wouldn't know how to put it together again, but he knew how all right, and, after an hour or so, there it was again, large and black and ugly, with a big screen on which all the lessons were shown and the questions were asked. That wasn't so bad. The part Margie hated most was the slot where she had to put homework and test papers. She always had to write them out in a punch code they made her learn when she was six years old, and the mechanical teacher calculated the mark in no time.

The Inspector had smiled after he was finished and patted

Margie's head. He said to her mother, 'It's not the little girl's fault, Mrs Jones. I think the geography sector was geared a little too quick. Those things happen sometimes. I've slowed it up to an average ten-year level. Actually, the over-all pattern of her progress is quite satisfactory.' And he patted Margie's head again.

Margie was disappointed. She had been hoping they would take the teacher away altogether. They had once taken Tommy's teacher away for nearly a month because the history sector had blanked out completely.

So she said to Tommy. 'Why would anyone write about school?'

Tommy looked at her with very superior eyes. 'Because it's not our kind of school, stupid. This is the old kind of school that they had hundreds and hundreds of years ago.' He added loftily, pronouncing the word carefully, '*Centuries* ago.'

Margie was hurt. 'Well, I don't know what kind of school they had all that time ago.' She read the book over his shoulder for a while, then said, 'Anyway, they had a teacher.'

'Sure they had a teacher, but it wasn't a *regular* teacher. It was a man.'

'A man? How could a man be a teacher?'

'Well, he just told the boys and girls things and gave them homework and asked them questions.'

'A man isn't smart enough.'

'Sure he is. My father knows as much as my teacher.'

'He can't. A man can't know as much as a teacher.'

'He knows almost as much, I betcha.'

Margie wasn't prepared to dispute that. She said, 'I wouldn't want a strange man in my house to teach me.'

Tommy screamed with laughter. 'You don't know much, Margie. The teachers didn't live in the house. They had a special building and all the kids went there.'

'And all the kids learned the same thing?'

'Sure, if they were the same age.'

'But my mother says a teacher has to be adjusted to fit the mind of each boy and girl it teaches and that each kid has to be taught differently.'

'Just the same they didn't do it that way then. If you don't like it, you don't have to read the book.'

'I didn't say I didn't like it,' Margie said quickly. She wanted to read about those funny schools.

They weren't even half finished when Margie's mother called, 'Margie! School!'

Margie looked up. 'Not yet, Mamma.'

'Now!' said Mrs Jones. 'And it's probably time for Tommy, too.'

Margie said to Tommy, 'Can I read the book some more with you after school?'

'Maybe,' he said, nonchalantly. He walked away whistling, the dusty old book tucked beneath his arm.

Margie went into the schoolroom. It was right next to her bedroom, and the mechanical teacher was on and waiting for her. It was always on at the same time every day except Saturday and Sunday, because her mother said little girls learned better if they learned at regular hours.

The screen was lit up, and it said: 'Today's arithmetic lesson is on the addition of proper fractions. Please insert yesterday's homework in the proper slot.'

Margie did so with a sigh. She was thinking about the old schools they had when her grandfather's grandfather was a little boy. All the kids from the whole neighbourhood came, laughing and shouting in the schoolyard, sitting together in the schoolroom, going home together at the end of the day. They learned the same things, so they could help one another on the homework and talk about it.

And the teachers were people . . .

The mechanical teacher was flashing on the screen: 'When we add the fractions ½ and ¼ – '

Margie was thinking about how the kids must have loved it in the old days. She was thinking about the fun they had.

ISAAC ASIMOV   The Earth is Room Enough

Talking about the passage

1 How is education in 2155 different from the way it is today?
2 What do you think are the advantages and disadvantages of the system of education used in 2155?
3 What might Margie have enjoyed about the type of school you attend?

Writing about the passage

1 Why were Margie and Tommy so fascinated with the book?
2 What had replaced books by 2155?
3 Why did Tommy think that the book was a waste?
4 How were the children taught?
5 Why did Margie hate school?

6   What was the County Inspector's job?
7   Why was Margie doubtful that a human could be a teacher?
8   Would you like to be taught in the same way as children in 2155? Give reasons for your answer.

Writing an account

Other writers have suggested how schools could still exist in the future. John Christopher has described how children on the Moon travel to a central school. He presents a history lesson in the school in the passage that follows:

They were doing the Roman Empire and Mr Milligan, the teacher, ran a reconstruct film on the screen. You saw a Roman family on the day of a Triumph, watching the yawning slaves prepare breakfast as the deep blue sky paled behind the roofs of the villa, heard the creak of ox-cart wheels in the narrow streets where the stone, through the long years, had worn into deep ruts . . . In schools on Earth, Marty gathered, reconstruct films gave you the smell of the scene in addition to sight and sound.

Write an account of 'A school of the future'. Before you start, list briefly the subjects that you think would be taught. Would they be taught in the same ways that they are at the moment? What buildings and facilities would the schools have?
You must plan your account carefully. Among the general approaches that you could use are the following:

1   Imagine that you attend such a school, and describe a day spent there.
2   Write a short handbook that the school might give to new pupils.
3   Imagine that you are a teacher in the school. Give your view of it.

Letter-writing

In the future space travel may become common. Colonies may be established on planets, like that on the moon in *The Lotus Caves*. Large stations could be built in space, where people would live and work for several years.

Imagine that you live in one of these space colonies, and write a letter to a friend on earth, describing the life you lead.

Further reading

In addition to *The Lotus Caves*, describing life on the moon and the discovery of 'the all-powerful Plant', John Christopher has written the following science-fiction novels:

The Guardians
Left alone at his father's death, Rob Randall escapes through the strong wire that divides the 'Conurb' from the old-fashioned but seemingly ideal 'County', only to find that the happy life there is preserved by inhuman means.

The Prince in Waiting, Beyond the Burning Lands and The Sword of the Spirits
These three novels tell of a time when earthquakes and volcanic eruptions have killed most of mankind, and only a few scattered human settlements remain.

You might enjoy the following novels by Nicholas Fisk:

The Space Hostages
This is the story of a secret spacecraft adrift in space, with nine children and a dying Flight Lieutenant on board.

Grinny
She appears from nowhere. She says she is Great Aunt Emma, but Tim and Beth soon realise that she is extremely dangerous and not even human.

Trillions
From the sky drift tiny, hard, shiny objects called 'Trillions', which seem to have strange powers.

8 Conversations

Good dialogue makes stories much more realistic. When a character speaks, his or her words have to be credible. They have to seem to be what that character would say in that situation. The speech should not interrupt the story, for the writer should tell part of the story through the dialogue.

'I want to report a murder.'

This passage is taken from Run for your Life *by David Line. The narrator, Woolcott, has gone to a London police station with a Hungarian boy, nicknamed Soldier.*

There were three or four policemen inside, without their helmets. They were doing things at filing cabinets and with ledgers. A sergeant was having a cup of tea at the main desk. He just cocked his eye at us over the cup.

'I want to report a murder,' Soldier said.

The sergeant put his cup down rather slowly. He had a moustache behind the cup and it twitched a bit.

'You want to do what?' he said.

'Report a murder.'

'Where?'

'I don't know where,' Soldier said.

'Who's been murdered?'

'Nobody yet,' Soldier said. 'That's what I want to tell you.'

Nobody said anything while he got it out. The other policemen stopped whatever they were doing and listened, too. The sergeant's moustache twitched a bit about half-way through and he started drinking his tea again. He didn't say anything for quite a while after Soldier had finished, and then he began drumming his fingers thoughtfully on the counter.

He said, 'Hm. This chap is a hunchback, is he?'

'Not completely hunched,' Soldier said. 'Just a bit hunched – because of his boot. His boot and his stick, you see.'

'His boot and his stick. And he wore thick glasses and had his hand covered so nobody could see it.'

'That's right,' Soldier said.

'M'hm. And these other fellows just went out and jumped on a number seven bus.'

'Not a number seven,' Soldier said. 'It was a five. A number five bus.'

'A number five?' the sergeant said, opening his eyes very wide. 'I thought you said a seven. I could have sworn you said a seven.'

I hadn't been certain of it to begin with because he'd kept his face straight, but I saw now he was laughing at Soldier. I felt my toes curling up.

'You see,' the sergeant said, 'we've got to be careful about your evidence because it's important. You're important, too, aren't you – I mean, you'd be about the only person for miles who could understand what they were saying, you being a Hungarian, too, eh?'

I said, 'He was the only one in that café who could, anyway.' I hadn't meant to speak, and I don't know why I did. I suppose it was the sight of Soldier stepping from one aching foot to the other and not even realizing he was being made fun of.

The sergeant gave me about half a minute of his moustache.
'And who might you be?' he said.
'I'm his friend.'

                        DAVID LINE   *Run for your Life*

Talking about the passage

1 What do we learn about the characters from the way that they speak?
2 What else does the writer tell the reader in the dialogue?
3 Have you ever found yourself in a situation where you could not convince someone that you were telling the truth? How did you feel? What did you do?

Writing about the passage

Answer the following questions in complete sentences and, as far as possible, in your own words.

1 Describe the scene in the police station when Woolcott and Soldier entered.
2 Why did the sergeant put his cup down slowly?
3 What caused the sergeant to say that the men boarded a number seven bus?
4 Why did Woolcott interrupt the conversation between Soldier and the sergeant?
5 What did the sergeant think of Soldier?
6 If you had been in the sergeant's place, what would you have thought of Soldier?
7 Write an account of an embarrassing interview involving a child and an adult.

Play-writing

Take the passage from *Run for your Life* and turn it into a scene from a radio play. Perhaps the best plays written could be tape-recorded. Put the name of the speaker beside the margin and separate it from the speech with a colon. For example the beginning of the play will be as follows:

SOLDIER: I want to report a murder.
SERGEANT: You want to do what?

SOLDIER: Report a murder.
SERGEANT: Where?
SOLDIER: I don't know where.
SERGEANT: Who's been murdered?
SOLDIER: Nobody yet. That's what I want to tell you.

When writing plays it is not necessary to put the spoken words in inverted commas, because the spoken and unspoken words are clearly divided and never appear in the same sentence.

Direct speech

When a sentence contains both spoken and unspoken words, they are separated by putting *inverted commas* around the spoken words:
'I want to report a murder,' Soldier said.

Inverted commas enclosing speech are always put after other punctuation marks:
'Not a number seven,' Soldier said. 'It was a five. A number five bus.'

Exercise 1

Rewrite the following passage, enclosing all spoken words in inverted commas.

Why are you late this morning? asked Mr James.
The bus was late, sir, Philip replied.
I thought you cycle to school, said Mr James suspiciously.
Yes, I do usually, answered Philip, but my bicycle has a puncture.
When did this puncture happen? asked Mr James, peering over his spectacles.
On Saturday, sir, said Philip, when I was going home from my aunt's.
You were late yesterday, too, said Mr James.
The bus was late yesterday as well, replied Philip. My dad says they're never on time.
But you, of course, were not on the bus, said Mr James. You told me yesterday that you were late because the chain had come off your bicycle as you were riding it to school. Do you think it was sensible to ride two miles with a flat tyre?

Spoken words are also divided from unspoken words in the same sentence by another punctuation mark.

It is usually a comma:
He asked, 'What is your name?'
'My name is Mary,' she replied.

It may, however, be a question mark or an exclamation mark:
'Where are you?' asked John.
'Over here!' shouted George.

Exercise 2

Rewrite the following passage, putting in any other punctuation marks that are needed.

What are you doing in that tree demanded the park-keeper
Inspecting it for woodworm said Joe Do you think it has Dutch Elm Disease
Probably not said the keeper as it is a beech tree
I can't see any sand replied Joe innocently
You're breaking the park rules said the keeper Why are you in that tree
Learning to fly retorted Joe
What do you think you are asked the keeper
Stuck said Joe

The first spoken word of a sentence begins with a capital letter, even if unspoken words come before it.
She said, 'It is not the same book.'

If unspoken words interrupt a spoken sentence, it is only the first word of the spoken sentence that takes a capital letter.
'It is,' she said, 'not the same book.'
'What differences,' he replied, 'are visible?'

Exercise 3

Rewrite the following sentences, putting capital letters wherever they are needed.

'the castle,' said the guide to his party, 'was built about 1080.'

'are there any dungeons in it?' asked theresa. 'are there any ghosts?'

'yes,' said the guide. 'the original floor is still visible in places.'

'will we see the dungeons?' demanded theresa.

'yes. the walls,' continued the guide, 'are fifteen feet thick.'

'when,' persisted theresa, 'will we see the dungeons?'

'soon. the stones,' he said, 'from which the walls were made were taken from ruined roman buildings.'

'but the dungeons,' said theresa, 'i want to see the dungeons.'

'certainly,' said the guide, 'this way.'

he opened a door and theresa hurried in.

'this door,' explained the guide, locking it, 'is four hundred years old and six inches thick.'

Exercise 4

Rewrite the following sentences, putting in punctuation marks and capital letters wherever they are needed.

1. the shop closes at five o'clock she said
2. he answered the train has already left
3. we asked him have you seen an old man with a dog
4. get out she shouted at me
5. does anyone of that name live here i asked
6. it is i said the first turning on the left
7. do you he asked have a spare pen
8. go away they shouted we have heard enough
9. where is he james asked i want to talk to him
10. the ship he said sank yesterday all the crew was drowned

Writing a conversation

When you are writing a conversation you should try to vary the verbs used. What alternatives can you think of for each of the following words:
said, asked, answered.

Write a short conversation which Woolcott and Soldier might have had after leaving the police station about what had happened inside. Take care to punctuate the conversation correctly and to vary the verbs used.

The woodwork lesson

The following passage is taken from another book by David Line. This time Woolcott is in school. He is telling the story himself, which is why the account contains conversational expressions.

'Woolcott!' It was Pike. He's the woodwork master, Pike. He picks on me. He's a twit. 'If you talked less and worked more, you'd get on better. What's this supposed to be?'

'It's a tie-rack, sir.'

He knew it was a tie-rack. I'd been making the flaming tie-rack for over a year. He hadn't let me take it home when the others took theirs: I'd sawn it wrong or planed it wrong or done something else wrong. It made me sick to look at it every week.

'Is that what it is? Is that what it is?' he said. He always repeats himself. He's an evil old swine. He blinks when he's excited. 'All you're doing, you're ruining wood. Know what wood this is? Know what it is, eh?'

'Mahogany, sir.'

'Yes. Mahogany. And planed against the grain, you little fool. What you think you're doing with it? What you doing with it, eh?'

'I'm making a tie-rack out of it,' I said.

Pike started to blink. 'Sir,' he said. 'Call me sir. Don't forget it. Don't forget it, eh?'

'All right,' I said. 'Sir.'

Just then someone said, 'Haw-haw-haw,' and Pike swung round.

'Who said that?' he said.

Nixon had said it. He'd been waggling his ears, too. Pike turned so fast he was still doing it. Nixon pretended he was scratching his ear.

'Nixon,' Pike said. 'It's you, Nixon.'

'Me, sir?' Nixon said. He looked down at himself. 'Why, yes, sir,' he said, a bit wonderingly. 'Of course it's me. Who else could it be, sir?'

Pike started blinking like mad. He's a bit scared of Nixon. Nixon's old man is one of the school governors. He's our doctor, Dr Nixon.

He said, 'Don't be cheeky, Nixon. That was you making that noise. I know it was.'

'Noise, sir?' Nixon said. 'I didn't hear any noise. Did you hear a noise?' he said to the kid next to him. The kid said he didn't, and in no time everyone was asking if they'd heard a noise. Nixon started taking a scientific interest in it. He asked Pike if it might have been the drains, or a bench creaking, or even Pike's digestion. Pike nearly went up the wall.

'What *kind* of noise was it, sir?' Nixon said, getting more interested every second.

He was trying to get Pike to make the noise himself, but Pike wasn't having any. The upshot was that Nixon got sent out, and I got sent out with him for laughing.

DAVID LINE *Mike and Me*

Talking about the passage

1 What do we learn about Mr Pike from the way he speaks?
2 How does Woolcott try to sound insolent?
3 What impression do we form of Nixon?

Writing about the passage

1 Why did Woolcott not like Mr Pike?
2 What made Mr Pike ask what the tie-rack was supposed to be?
3 Why had Woolcott been making it for such a long time?
4 How did Nixon first try to make a fool of Mr Pike?
5 Why was Mr Pike a little afraid of Nixon?
6 How did this fear show?
7 When Nixon had been caught, how did he go on annoying Mr Pike?

Vocabulary

A *prefix* is a part of a word which is added in front of the root to affect its meaning. For instance, the Greek prefix *arch-*, meaning 'chief' may be used to form words such as '*arch*angel' (meaning 'chief angel'), '*arch*bishop' (meaning 'chief bishop') and '*arch*deacon', (meaning 'chief deacon').

1 Try to find the meanings of the prefixes *tele* and *trans*, then trace the meanings of the following groups of words:
   a telecast, telecommunication, telepathy, telephone, telephotography, teleprinter, telescope, television.
   b transatlantic, transcontinental, transfer, transform, transgress, translate, transmit, transoceanic, transparent, transplant, transport, transpose.

Writing a story

Describe an occasion when a pupil, perhaps yourself, was in trouble with a teacher or someone else in authority. Tell the story mainly through dialogue, remembering to begin a new paragraph whenever the speaker changes. Before you start, form a clear idea of the situation and imagine carefully the characters of the two speakers. Try to bring out the sounds of their voices and their feelings in what you write. When you are checking and revising your rough draft, ask yourself how effectively the dialogue has been used, and how accurately the characters of the speakers are shown by what they say.

Adverbs

An *adverb* is a word which tells us how, when or where the action of a verb takes place.

In the following sentence an adverb of manner tells us how the action is carried out:
*The boy ran **quickly**.*
Most adverbs that explain how an action is carried out end in the suffix *-ly*.

In this sentence an adverb of time tells us *when* the action was carried out:
*She arrived **today**.*

The last example is of an adverb of place which tells us *where* the action was carried out:
*He drove **there**.*

Exercise 5

Rewrite the following sentences, underlining the adverbs which they contain.

1. The stranger spoke rapidly and was difficult to understand.
2. He gazed at the man suspiciously as he had seen him before.
3. Yesterday I met an old friend and recognised her immediately.
4. She was there, and she greeted me warmly.
5. The dog ran swiftly and soon reached the gate.
6. He had been there and had already opened the door.
7. They then asked him to give a reply hastily.
8. The empty house decayed gradually.
9. Tomorrow I hope to go shopping and I intend to start early.
10. The rain fell heavily and the gale blew fiercely.

Dialogue is usually written for characters but in Russell Edson's work the speakers are often objects. Food, for example, can talk to the person planning to eat it, and furniture can answer its owners back.

A landscape tale

A gravy boat had run aground, and now gravy was spilling through the landscape.
A treadmill making its way through the landscape saw a couple of onions floating on a dark gravy.

Hello sirs, said the treadmill.

The onions not used to speaking to strangers continued floating along with the gravy.

I say sirs, said the treadmill, there's been a bit of trouble in the landscape; it seems a steam organ stomped its master to death . . .

Oh well, thought the treadmill, I suppose the little sirs have better things to do than talk with strangers.

The gravy was lost. It thought it saw lights through the trees, but they were only stars.

The little onions cried, are we going to the stars?

Hush, said the gravy.

Now they heard music. The little onions cried, music and laughter.

Oh I could use a little laughter, said the gravy.

And so the gravy began to spill towards the music.

The little onions were crying, hurry, hurry.

As the treadmill was crossing a bridge out of the landscape it heard carnival music; and there below the bridge the ferocious steam organ was sucking the gravy up into its pipes. The little onions were screaming.

Ah, said the treadmill, I miss my little glockenspiel. And the treadmill continued over the bridge, the one that connects this landscape to the reader.

RUSSELL EDSON

Even when this writer used human characters, the dialogue he produced was strange.

When the ceiling cries

A mother tosses her infant so that it hits the ceiling.

Father says, why are you doing that to the ceiling?

Do you want my baby to fly away to heaven? The ceiling is there so that the baby will come back to me, says mother.

Father says, you are hurting the ceiling, can't you hear it crying?

So mother and father climb a ladder and kiss the ceiling.

RUSSELL EDSON

You must have noticed that Russell Edson has not put the spoken words inside inverted commas, nor has he always begun the first word of a spoken sentence with a capital letter. Copy out the poems, punctuating them in the usual way.

Writing your own poem

Write a nonsense poem which includes a conversation. The speakers may be human or objects, or a mixture of both.

Further reading

David Line has written:

Run for your Life
Serialised on television as *Soldier and Me*, this is a story filled with suspense. Jim Woolcott befriends a small Hungarian boy who has been forced to flee from his native country, and who is in danger after discovering a murder plot.

Mike and Me
Jim Woolcott and his cousin, Mike, investigate the mysterious fire which breaks out in Lepic, the picture-framer's gallery. This leads them into a tense and dangerous adventure which also involves their friend, Soldier, and 'Moggy', their art master.

9 The supernatural

The 'atmosphere' of a piece of writing is the feeling that it suggests. Stories and poems can create a mood in the reader.

The most favourable time to read a supernatural story is a winter's evening, when it is dark outside and inside an open fire is casting shadows on the walls of a dimly-lit room. The skilful writer of supernatural stories, however, does not need the right setting in order to have his or her stories believed. The well-written tale has the right effect on its readers, even if they read it on a sunny morning.

This unit contains two passages dealing with the supernatural. The first extract treats it humorously. The second is more serious, and carefully builds up an atmosphere. Both passages show the value of putting supernatural events into a world made to seem realistic by the detail in which it is presented.

The haunting

Mr and Mrs Harrison and their family had moved into a cottage which was haunted by the ghost of a seventeenth-century sorcerer, Thomas Kempe. Only James Harrison and his dog, Tim, were aware that the ghost was the cause of the strange happenings in the cottage, such as when the Vicar called. The Vicar noticed Tim, that had begun to show that he knew Thomas Kempe was present in the room.

'Dear me, how like the stray who got in and took the joint from our larder last week. Curious to see two mongrels so much alike, eh? Well, well. And how's school, young man?'

'Fine,' said James, 'thanks.' Tim was struggling violently, and lunging with bared teeth at a point somewhere behind the Vicar. The windows rattled. 'These autumn winds,' said the Vicar. 'I always think of those at sea.'

'What?' said Mrs Harrison. 'Oh, yes, yes, quite.' She slammed the lid on the teapot irritably.

The electric light flickered. Upstairs, distantly, came the sound of an alarm clock going off. A cup jinked in its saucer on the dresser.

'Do sit down,' said Mrs Harrison. 'James, pull up a chair for the Vicar.'

James fetched the windsor chair from the corner and placed it by the table. He still had one hand on its arm as the Vicar began to lower himself into it, and so felt the whole thing twitch, stagger, and jerk suddenly sideways, so that the Vicar, prodded violently in the hip, lurched against the table and almost fell.

'James!' said Mrs Harrison angrily. 'Look what you're doing!'

'Sorry,' said James in confusion, straightening the chair. The Vicar sat down, rubbing his hip and also apologizing. Tim began to bark hysterically.

'Put that dog out!' shouted Mrs Harrison.

With Tim outside, things were quieter, except for another bang as the back door, this time, slammed. The Vicar passed a hand across his forehead and rubbed his head, furtively.

'Family life, eh! There's always something going on, what?'

'Never a dull moment,' said Mrs Harrison grimly. 'Milk?'

'Oh – please – yes, if I may . . . So kind of you. I do hope I'm not interrupting. I'm sure you're very busy, like we all are these days, eh?'

'Not at all,' said Mrs Harrison. 'James, pass the Vicar his tea, will you?'

James, with extreme caution, carried cup and saucer across the room. He was standing in front of the Vicar, and the Vicar's fingers were just closing on the edge of the saucer, when the cup jolted, tipped, hung at an angle of forty-five degrees, and turned over. Tea flowed into the saucer, and thence in a cascade on to the Vicar's trousers.

'James!' said Mrs Harrison in a strangled voice.

PENELOPE LIVELY   *The Ghost of Thomas Kempe*

Talking about the passage

1 What does the dialogue tell us about the characters in this passage?
2 How does the ghost show its presence in this scene?
3 Where does the humour come from in the passage?

Writing about the passage

Answer questions 1 to 5 in sentences and, as far as possible, in your own words.

1. Of what was the Vicar reminded when he saw Tim?
2. How did the Vicar explain the rattling of the windows?
3. What happened when James pulled up a chair for the Vicar?
4. Why was it necessary to put Tim outside?
5. Describe the feelings of James, Mrs Harrison and the Vicar at the end of the passage.
6. Give a word or phrase which means the same as each of the following as it is used in the passage:
   irritably, hysterically, furtively, cascade.
7. There are many verbs of action in this passage. Explain precisely the movements suggested by the following verbs:
   jinked, twitch, stagger, jerk, lurched, jolted.

Play-writing

A 'poltergeist' is a ghost that moves things around and throws things, as Thomas Kempe's ghost does. Imagine that a family has gone to live in an old house. One evening they come to suspect that the house is haunted by a poltergeist. Write a short radio play about that evening.

Before you begin, decide on your characters. Consider what each is like, the way he or she would speak, and how he or she would react to the mysterious events. Give the play an exciting opening. The ghost's activities should become increasingly noticeable until a climax is reached. Try to give your play an effective ending.

Set out the play as you did the radio play based on the extract from *Run for your Life*. Put any sound effects in brackets. Perhaps you will be able to tape-record your play for others to hear.

Subject and predicate

A sentence may be divided into two parts, the *subject* and the *predicate*. The subject tells us what the sentence is about. The predicate tells us something about the subject, usually what the subject does or what the subject is.

To find the subject of a sentence you should look for the verb. When you have found it, ask yourself who or what is carrying out the action.

The electric light flickered.

In this sentence the verb is 'flickered'. If you ask who or what flickered, the answer is 'the electric light', so the subject is 'the electric light'. If you ask what the electric light did, the answer is 'flickered', so 'flickered' is the predicate. The sentence may be divided as follows:

> **Subject**   **Predicate**
> The electric light   flickered.

In the sentence
A cup jinked in its saucer on the dresser.
the verb is 'jinked'. If you ask who or what jinked, the answer is 'a cup' so the subject is 'a cup'. If you ask what a cup did, the answer is 'jinked in its saucer on the dresser', so this is the predicate. The sentence may be divided as follows:

> **Subject**   **Predicate**
> A cup   jinked in its saucer on the dresser.

The main word of a subject is a noun or a pronoun. The main word of a predicate is a verb.

Exercise 1

Divide a page into two columns, labelling one 'subject' and the other 'predicate'. Rewrite the following sentences, dividing them correctly between the two columns.

1 The windows rattled.
2 I always think of those at sea.
3 She slammed the lid on the teapot irritably.
4 The Vicar sat down, rubbing his hip and also apologizing.
5 Tim began to bark hysterically.
6 James, with extreme caution, carried cup and saucer across the room.
7 Tea flowed into the saucer, and thence in a cascade onto the Vicar's trousers.
8 Lucy had always wanted a four-poster bed.
9 They still had the faint spicy smell of last year's lavender.
10 The murmuring voices filled her head.

Exercise 2

Add predicates to the following subjects to make complete sentences.

1   the tree
2   the grey car
3   the sea
4   the house at the top of the hill
5   the three horses
6   the girl in the green dress
7   an old lady and her dog
8   a man with a limp
9   the town by the sea
10 my uncle and aunt

By St Thomas Water

By St Thomas Water
Where the river is thin
We looked for a jam-jar
To catch the quick fish in.
Through St Thomas Church-yard
Jessie and I ran
The day we took the jam-pot
Off the dead man.

On the scuffed tombstone
The grey flowers fell,
Cracked was the water,
Silent the shell.
The snake for an emblem
Swirled on the slab,
Across the beach of sky the sun
Crawled like a crab.

'If we walk,' said Jessie,
'Seven times round,
We shall hear a dead man
Speaking underground.'
Round the stone we danced, we sang,
Watched the sun drop,
Laid our heads and listened
At the tomb-top.

Soft as the thunder
At the storm's start
I heard a voice as clear as blood,
Strong as the heart.
But what words were spoken
I can never say,
I shut my fingers round my head,
Drove them away.

'What are those letters, Jessie,
Cut so sharp and trim
All round this holy stone
With earth up to the brim?'
Jessie traced the letters
Black as coffin-lead.
'He is not dead but sleeping,'
Slowly she said.

I looked at Jessie,
Jessie looked at me,
And our eyes in wonder
Grew wide as the sea.
Past the green and bending stones
We fled hand in hand,
Silent through the tongues of grass
To the river strand.

By the creaking cypress
We moved as soft as smoke
For fear all the people
Underneath awoke.
Over all the sleepers
We darted light as snow
In case they opened up their eyes,
Called us from below.

Many a day has faltered
Into many a year
Since the dead awoke and spoke
And we would not hear.
Waiting in the cold grass
Under a crinkled bough,
Quiet stone, cautious stone,
What do you tell me now?

CHARLES CAUSLEY

Talking about the poem

1. What is the atmosphere of the poem?
2. How does the poet create this atmosphere?
3. Why did the children go to the churchyard?
4. What happened when they carried out the ritual?
5. Why did the children run away?
6. The poet uses many comparisons. Why does he choose the comparisons listed below?
   - a Across the beach of sky the sun
        Crawled like a crab
   - b We fled hand in hand,
        Silent through the tongues of grass
   - c We moved as soft as smoke

d We darted light as snow.

Similes

A comparison in which one thing is said to be like or as something else is called a *simile*.

For example, the following lines contain three similes:

Soft as the thunder
At the storm's start
I heard a voice as clear as blood,
Strong as the heart.

Some similes have been used so often that they no longer have any power to make the listener imagine the two things compared. Such similes include:

as quiet as a mouse
as cold as ice
as white as snow.

To be effective a simile should be unusual. When Charles Causley wanted to describe the letters on the tombstone he could have called them 'as black as coal' or 'as black as soot', but this would have made little impact upon his reader. It was far more striking for him to say that the letters were 'black as coffin-lead'. Why?

Exercise 3

Complete each of the following similes in a way that is effective and unusual.

1. as silent as
2. as hot as
3. as green as
4. as happy as
5. as smooth as
6. as blue as
7. as rare as
8. as sharp as
9. as new as
10. as old as

Writing your own poem

In *By St Thomas Water* Charles Causley has described an experience in a very clear and vivid way. Remember a particular experience from your past. You may have been alone, or with a friend or a group of friends. The experience should be connected with a certain place, perhaps one which you had never known before, or which you had rarely visited. The place might be a garden or a building.

Describe the experience and express your feelings about it in a poem. Make the poem simple, but try to write vividly, being especially careful over your choice of words and similes. Prepare a draft of your poem, and then look at it very carefully and critically. Be ruthless in changing it if you feel it is necessary. When you are completely satisfied, and this might be only after several drafts, write out your final copy of the poem.

Direct speech

When a new speaker begins to talk, you should start a new paragraph.

'James!' said Mrs Harrison angrily. 'Look what you're doing!'
'Sorry,' said James in confusion, straightening the chair. The Vicar sat down, rubbing his hip and also apologizing. Tim began to bark hysterically.
'Put that dog out!' shouted Mrs Harrison.

Rewrite the following passage, beginning a new paragraph each time the speaker changes.

'Where have you been today?' Mrs French asked her son. 'I went out with some friends,' Ken replied. 'But where did you go?' his mother persisted. After a pause he answered, 'To the woods.' 'I told you not to go there,' said Mrs French, annoyed. 'Why did you go when I had told you not to?' 'The others were going,' he replied rather sullenly. 'I thought you meant I was not to go there alone.' 'What did you do there?' she asked. 'Nothing much. We climbed a few trees,' he answered. 'You didn't go to the old cottage,' she said, looking at him carefully. 'No,' he answered, after hesitating, with a guilty look on his face. 'You did, didn't you?' his mother said sternly.

Writing a conversation

Imagine and write the conversation the Vicar had with his wife after he returned home from his visit to the Harrisons' house, described in the extract from *The Ghost of Thomas Kempe*.

Long-ago voices

A widow becomes caretaker of a large empty house which is said to be haunted. She lives in a cottage in the grounds with her children. Her daughter, Lucy, likes to explore the building.

And yet . . . if the ghosts were not to be seen, she felt sometimes that she could almost hear them. Even now, as she sat in the April sunlight, her ears seemed to catch the faintest sighing of long-ago voices, a dim murmuring as though generations of people were all talking at once but very softly. As she sat listening, her mind drifted and the voices seemed to grow louder, with here and there a word that was clear . . . or very nearly so. And then it seemed that the sounds reached her ears from inside, like a roaring in her head that frightened her so that she rose up from the window seat and hurried away, clattering along the stone passage and up the wide staircase until the noise of her feet drove the voices away.

    She moved along the first-floor landing and opened the third door on the left. This was her favourite bedroom with a small four-poster bed hung with faded pink curtains. Lucy had always wanted a four-poster bed. She wished that she could sleep in it just once instead of in the little white bedstead in her room in the caretaker's cottage. She opened the dark wooden chest where blankets waited for the bed to be made up again. They still had the faint spicy smell of last year's lavender. I'll ask mother if I can, she thought, just once. But suppose she woke in the night and saw a lady in grey go gliding through the wall? Nonsense, she told herself, there are no such things . . . But she closed the door gently as she went out.

    She climbed the small twisting stairs where scores of housemaids had come and gone: yawning sleepily in the cold light of dawn as they went down to black the grates; yawning wearily by the light of their candlesticks as they went up again at the end of a long day. High under the roof were their little bedrooms with sloping ceilings, but these had not been used for a long time and they had a forlorn neglected air. Lucy longed to make curtains for the tiny windows, to paste back the wallpaper where it hung down from the walls. She hoped when they found the owners that they would have children to live and play in these little rooms at the top of the house. Whenever the murmuring voices filled her head, it was always the clear, high voices of children that she caught most distinctly.

ANTONIA BARBER *The Ghosts*

Talking about the passage

1 What is the atmosphere of the passage?
2 Which words and details help to suggest the atmosphere?
3 Where has the writer chosen words that represent sounds?
4 Do you believe in ghosts? Give reasons for your answer.

Writing about the passage

Answer questions 1 to 6 in complete sentences, using your own words as far as possible.

1 Describe the sounds that Lucy heard.
2 How did she stop herself from hearing the sounds?
3 What made Lucy want to sleep in her favourite bedroom, and what made her doubtful about sleeping there?
4 Why did she close the door gently?
5 Whom did Lucy picture on the stairs?
6 What changes would Lucy have liked for the small bedrooms under the roof?
7 Give words or phrases which mean the same as the following words:
forlorn, neglected, distinctly.

Vocabulary

A *suffix* is a part of a word which is added after the root to change its meaning. For example, the suffix *-able*, means 'capable of being' and may be used to form such adjectives as 'cur*able*' (capable of being cured) and 'desir*able*' (capable of being desired). Can you think of any other words using this suffix?

The Latin suffix *-fy* and the English *-en* are both suffixes meaning 'make' and are used to form verbs.

1   Explain the meanings of the following verbs:
    a   amplify, clarify, electrify, fortify, liquefy, magnify, modify, mystify, sanctify, solidify.
    b   brighten, dampen, darken, frighten, lengthen, lighten, shorten, soften, strengthen, widen.
2   The suffix *-ise* or *-ize* also means 'make'. How many verbs can you think of that use this suffix?

Letter-writing

You have gone to stay at the house of a friend or relative. While you are there, you begin to suspect that the house is haunted, yet you do not feel that you can tell your host or hostess. Write a letter to a close friend, explaining your fears and their causes.

Writing a story

Imagine that, while you are out walking alone, you see a gate in a wall. Something causes you to open it. What do you find on the other side? A garden? A forest? Another world? Write a story called 'Through the gate'.

Before you begin, decide on the atmosphere that you want to suggest. Perhaps you want to arouse a feeling of happiness, sadness, peacefulness, mystery, wonder or menace. Try to suggest the atmosphere strongly as you write. Describe carefully what you see, hear, smell and imagine.

Further reading

Penelope Lively has written the following books:

The Ghost of Thomas Kempe
James is plagued by the ghost of a sorcerer, and it becomes vital for James to exorcise the spirit.

The Driftway
The Driftway is an ancient road on which those with ears to hear pick up messages from the past. This is what happens to Paul, who is running away from home. He encounters an Anglo-Saxon boy, a young Roundhead from the Civil War, and an eighteenth-century

highwayman amongst others who help him to solve his own problems.

The Wild Hunt of Hagworthy
Lucy and Kester witness the revival of an ancient ritual dance in a Somerset village. Legend and reality grow together into a vivid and frightening climax.

The Whispering Knights
Three children try a little amateur witchcraft and evoke an evil which threatens the village as well as themselves.

Astercote
A few miles from Oxford two children stumble on the remains of a village that died with the Black Death.

The House in Norham Gardens
Clare, living in a vast Victorian house with her two old aunts and two unusual lodgers, is disturbed by a gaudily-painted shield that she finds in the attic. The brown men who flit in and out of her dreams seem to want something from her, but what?

Going Back
Jane returns with her two children to the house she was brought up in and remembers the adventures, joys and fear that she and her companion, Edward, experienced in the same village during World War II.

A Stitch in Time
Maria is spending her holiday in a Victorian house in Lyme Regis. The unexplained noises of a creaking swing and a yapping dog which does not exist, and the mysterious effect of Harriet, who once lived in the house, turn her holiday into a tense and dramatic jigsaw, which is not pieced together until the final chapter.

10 Summer and swallows

Looking back

At the beginning of this final unit, it is useful to remind you of the main pieces of advice that you have been given in *Englishcraft 1*.

- Remember the readers for whom you are writing.
- Be your most critical reader, particularly when checking your rough drafts.
- Imagine and write in detail.
- Use your senses.
- Plan your stories carefully, beginning and ending effectively so that you gain and keep your reader's interest.
- Build each story around a main incident.
- Deal with characters you know.
- Use dialogue purposefully.
- Read thoughtfully and widely, learning from examples.

Re-read the stories and poems that you have written this year. Where have you made progress? What further improvements would you like to make? If any are needed try to make some in your work *now* as you complete this unit.

Like a cork

Lucy Graham decided to go for a swim by herself. She walked down the beach, enjoying the feeling of the sand beneath her feet. She stopped to tie back her hair.

Then she ran on, into the water that was no more at first than a change in texture, turning the sand from warm to less warm, to cool, and then at last to chill. She pulled in her breath and ran on until the sea was dragging at her knees. A few more yards and she was able to plunge in.
 Even on that day the cold of the Atlantic made her gasp. She struck out boldly and soon the sun on her head and neck warmed

her again, and the water was no longer cold, only soft and buoyant and beautiful.

The Grahams were all good swimmers, but Lucy was the best. Her father had taught her when she was only five, and she had won medals and two silver cups. She had no difficulty in getting herself round the little headland into the triangle of water between the reef's two outstretched arms. Already she had a sight of her father and Sarah, unsuspecting and relaxed as they sat together on the shore. It was as she smiled to think how she would surprise them that she was surprised herself. A long swelling wave broke over the tip of the reef and rolled her in between the two arms, in a lazy and apparently friendly fashion. Then it pulled right back again and took her with it.

That saved her trouble, but it carried her much too far. She struck out for the shore confidently enough, then knew in a matter of seconds that she was making no progress at all.

Lucy looked about her but no other swimmers were within reach. In fact she realised at once that they were all either north or south of the reef, as though they knew the difficulties of the water in between. For a moment she panicked, feeling like a cork in the deceptively gentle sea, knowing all too well how easily she might be swept further and further out – terrifyingly aware that no one even knew she was there.

She rested and steadied herself before trying again. Resting was not a good thing in one way, for the moment she relaxed she was swept helplessly on the swell. She closed her eyes tight for a second and tried to draw in strength and good sense to herself. She could not believe that this was happening to her, and even though she was frightened she managed to be angry, too, at her own stupidity.

BARBARA WILLARD   *The Battle of Wednesday Week*

Talking about the passage

1   Is Lucy overconfident regarding her power as a swimmer?
2   In what way does the sentence below add to the tension in the passage?
    'Already she had a sight of her father and Sarah, unsuspecting and relaxed as they sat together on the shore.'
3   What other factors contribute to the tension?
4   Does Lucy react sensibly to the danger? If you had been Lucy, what would you have done next?

Writing about the passage

Answer the questions in sentences and, as far as possible, in your own words.

1 Describe the stretch of coastline where Lucy was swimming.
2 Had Lucy told her father or Sarah that she was going for a swim? Give a reason for your answer.
3 What was the effect of the wave that broke over the tip of the reef?
4 When did Lucy realise that she was in danger?
5 What did Lucy do after she had become aware of the danger?
6 Why was Lucy angry as well as frightened?
7 What lessons about swimming in the sea could be learned from reading this extract?

Writing a description

Look carefully at the photograph showing a beach in winter. What details do you notice? What further details are you able to imagine?
   How would the same beach look in summer?

When you have made detailed notes on what you would see, hear, smell and feel if you were in that place at those times, write a description called 'The beach', contrasting the beach and its atmosphere in summer and winter.

You might choose to approach the description from the point of view of someone who lives near the place, or from that of someone who visits it occasionally, perhaps for a particular reason.

Subject and predicate

Usually the subject comes at the beginning of a sentence, but this is not always the case.

Swimming powerfully, he approached the shore.
Here the verb is 'approached'. When we ask who or what approached, the answer is 'he', so 'he' is the subject. The sentence may be divided in the following way:

Subject	**Predicate**
He	approached the shore swimming powerfully

At the end of the pier the two boys stopped.
Here the verb is 'stopped'. When we ask who or what stopped, the answer is 'the two boys', so this is the subject. The sentence may be divided as follows:

Subject	**Predicate**
The two boys	stopped at the end of the pier.

Exercise 1

Divide the following sentences into subject and predicate.

1. Shouting loudly, they ran across the beach.
2. Along the promenade the girl walked.
3. Sweeping over the sandcastles, the waves reached the deck chairs.
4. Beginning to panic, the swimmer felt the current's pull.
5. Seeing the scattered food, a flock of seagulls gathered.
6. Over the sparkling water sailed the first yacht.
7. At two o'clock the dolphin show began.

8   After two hours the man awoke to find the sea near.
9   On the deserted beach a bucket and spade had been left.
10 Tomorrow most of the people on holiday will leave for home.

When you divide a question into subject and predicate, it is advisable to treat the sentence as if it were a statement.
Are you going in the water?
If we turn this question into a statement, we have,
You are going in the water.
The verb is 'are going' and the subject is 'you'. The question may be divided in the following way:

Subject	*Predicate*
You	*are going in the water.*

Orders do not always include the subject, which is usually 'you'.
Stop at once!
Here the verb is 'stop' and the subject 'you' is not actually said. When you divide an order into subject and predicate, the subject is given, but if it is unstated it is put in brackets.

Subject	*Predicate*
(You)	*Stop at once.*

Exercise 2

Divide the following questions and orders into subject and predicate.

1   Can the boat be repaired?
2   Watch out for jellyfish!
3   Is this the best spot for swimming?
4   Have you brought any suntan lotion?
5   Stay away from the breakwater!
6   At what time will the tide be in?
7   Are you going to stay here all day?
8   Is the lost child wearing a red shirt?
9   Stop splashing your little sister!
10 Was the broken glass left on the beach?

Remember that, with the exception of orders, every sentence must have a subject and a predicate.

The arrival

Our train steams slowly in, and we creep to a stop at last.
There's a great unlatching of doors, and the coaches, emptying fast,
Let loose their loads of children, and mothers with talkative friends,
And sandwiches, flasks, and push-chairs, and apples, and odds and ends.

And we move in a crowd together, amid churns and trolleys and crates,
Along by a cobbled courtyard, and out through the station gates;
We pass by the waiting taxis; then turn a corner and reach
To where with its flags and cafés the road curves down to the beach.

We move in the livelier air, between shining shops and stalls;
Never was such a confusion of coloured bright beach-balls,
And plastic buckets and boats, and ducks of a rubbery blue,
And strings of sandals, and stacks of rock-with-the-name-right-through!

Till the many smells which beset us – of onions and cooking greens,
Of fumes from the cars and 'buses, of smoke from the noisy inns –
All merge in the one large gust which blows on us broad and free,
And catches us, throat and limbs, and heart – the smell of the sea!

JOHN WALSH

Talking about the poem

1. How does the poet contrast the arrival of the train with the exit of the holidaymakers?
2. How realistic is the poet's description of the scene at the station?
3. In what ways is the air 'livelier' as the crowd moves closer to the beach?
4. What details of the stalls does the poet mention?
5. Describe the distinctive smell which he remembered.
6. What sights, sounds and smells do you associate with a day at the seaside?
7. Explain why you would or would not like to be one of the crowd in John Walsh's poem.

Holiday towns

Not all holiday centres are at the seaside. Two towns that are popular with tourists are described below. One is a seaside town, but the other is inland.

Gloucester

One of England's oldest cities, Gloucester is situated in the Vale of Severn between the Cotswolds and the Forest of Dean. It has an imposing cathedral, a lively market, fine new shopping areas and walkways linking buildings of historic interest with those of a more modern design. A Severnside harbour gives the city a distinctive character. Population 91 000

Touring: The Cotswolds; Forest of Dean; Wye Valley; Vale of Severn; Malvern Hills.

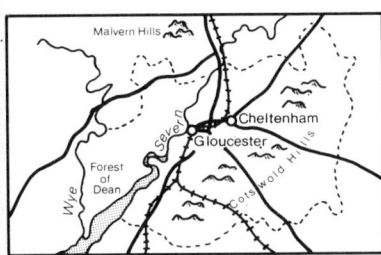

Amenities: Leisure Centre, including swimming pools, sports facilities; cinema; county cricket ground; parks; greyhound track.

Some events: *Tredworth Annual Road Race,* Easter Monday; *Longford Annual Road Walk,* Spring Bank Holiday; *Cheese Rolling Ceremony,* Spring Bank Holiday; *Cricket Festival,* June; *Gloucester Festival,* September.

Rail: Gloucester Central.

Road: Express Coach Service.

Whitley Bay & Tynemouth
Tyne & Wear

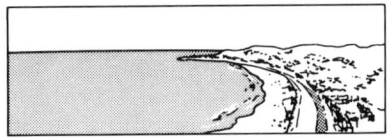

The twin resorts at the Gateway to Northumbria offer four miles of clean golden sands stretching from the Tyne pier northwards to St Mary's Island. Plenty of room for everyone and fun for all the family!

Beaches: Sweeping bays and sheltered coves; abundance of rock pools.

Touring: The ancient kingdom of Northumbria, all within day-trip distance.

Amenities: Funfair; indoor leisure pool with waves etc.; outdoor pool on the beach; golf; tennis; boating; putting; bowls; markets; nightlife; Priory; Castle; fishing port.

Some events: *International Folk Moot Week,* July; *Carnival Fortnight,* July 22nd - August 6th; *Whitley Bay Show,* August Bank Holiday Weekend.

Rail: Frequent services from Newcastle.

Road: Frequent services from Newcastle.

For discussion

- Explain the main differences between the two towns.
- What might attract visitors to Gloucester? Who might go there for a holiday?
- What might attract visitors to Whitley Bay and Tynemouth?

- Who might go there for a holiday?
- In which of the towns would you prefer to spend a holiday? Give reasons for your choice.
- What other information might have been included in the descriptions?

Writing an article

Write a description for a travel magazine of your town or area, or a town near to where you live. You will want to present your subject in such a way as to encourage people to visit it.

What aspects of the town or area will you emphasise?

You may set out your description in the same way as the two examples given above, but add extra information and subheadings if you wish.

Writing your own poem

Imagine that you have spent a day at the seaside, perhaps on the beach shown on page 137. It is now time to make your way to the carpark, coach or railway station. Write a poem called 'The departure'.

As you plan your poem, consider the following questions:

1. What would your feelings be as you leave the beach?
2. In what ways would the appearance of the seaside town differ from the appearance it had in the morning?
3. How could your poem appeal to the senses?
4. Which other details could you include?
5. What comparisons would make your description vivid to the reader?

Make notes of your main ideas before you start. When you have written your draft, carefully revise it, then make a final copy.

The boat

Madge and Paul have gone to stay with their grandmother, who lives at the seaside. The two children are playing in the sea. Paul visited the beach the previous night, and said that he did not feel that he was alone there.

'Are you all right, Paul?' calls Madge, over the waves.

'No! Drowned, drowned!' he shouts back, and not seeing the big wave come, goes under again. He rises to Madge, wading, struggling with deep heavy legs towards her. Seeing him all right she pretends at once that she was only coming to chase him, but he knows. 'Fusspot!' he calls.

Later they lie in the soft sand to dry, and look at the great cloud-castles wheeling by, and the gulls drifting circles in the depths of the sky. 'You are right about it feeling different, Paul,' says Madge.

'I feel watched.'

'There's nobody here,' he says. 'Shall we look at the boat now?'

'Yes, now.' Madge says. We always have to come round to it slowly, she thinks, I wonder why. It has something to do with liking it so much. I don't understand me.

The boat lies tilted slightly, slightly submerged in the sand. Sand has washed inside it, and settled there, giving it a smooth beachy floor. Its sides are festooned with the necklace-of-beads sort of seaweed that pops when you squeeze its bubbles. Lower down it is livid with the bright green weedy slime that covers the sea-washed rocks. And yet it is all in one piece, and still riding on its rusty chain, though it is the slope of the beach it rides now, not the tilting sea. But the winter has left its mark. Most of the boat is bleached grey, weathered down. Deep cracks run along every grain of the once living wood, and it has a pale worn smoothness, like leprosy. Running fingers over it finds ups and downs like bones. A little paint still holds on it. It was turquoise blue paint, all crazed along the cracks in the wood, and mostly flaked away, so that what remains are little lines of it, curling at the edges, and bright against the pale wood. Madge scratches at the raised edge of a piece with her fingernail, and at once the whole flake lifts off.

'Could we paint it blue again, Paul?' she asks.

JILL PATON WALSH *Goldengrove*

Talking about the passage

1 Why do you think Jill Paton Walsh chose to write this passage in the present tense?
2 What are Madge's feelings about Paul at the opening of the passage? Why does she pretend she was chasing him?
3 Why do you think Madge wants to paint the boat?
4 What details does the writer use to make the scene vivid?

Writing about the passage

Answer the following questions in complete sentences and, as far as possible, in your own words.

1 Why does Paul call Madge a 'fusspot'?
2 How does Madge feel that the beach has changed this morning?
3 Describe the boat.
4 How has winter affected it?
5 Why do Madge and Paul like the boat?

6 Explain how the boat might be restored.
7 Give a word or phrase which means the same as each of the following words as it is used in the passage:
submerged, livid, crazed.

Writing a story

Here are two quotations taken from extracts which appear in this unit:

1 'She could not believe that this was happening to her, and even though she was frightened she managed to be angry, too, at her own stupidity.'
2 'You are right about it feeling different, Paul,' says Madge. 'I feel watched.'

Either of these quotations could be the starting point for an exciting story. Choose one and write a story, using the quotation as its opening. If you choose the second quotation what will you have to remember about tenses?

Revision of punctuation

Exercise 3

Rewrite the following sentences, putting in capital letters and punctuation marks wherever they are needed.

1 the beach was crowded as the day was hot
2 where would be the best place for the family to sit
3 it was the first time catherine aged one had been to portstewart
4 she had a blue bucket a red spade and several moulds for shaping sand
5 she built sandcastles demolished them dug holes and filled them in
6 after a while however she wanted to paddle in the sea
7 she wanted her sisters sarah and helen to go with her
8 catherine wasnt afraid as she approached the seas edge
9 the cold water swept around catherines feet
10 she laughed to see the waves large and rough breaking noisily

Exercise 4

Rewrite the following passage, putting in capital letters and punctuation marks wherever they are needed.

   have you seen roger asked mrs cannon
jeremy replied i havent
   i thought he had come on the pier to meet you said mrs cannon becoming worried
   he told me yesterday answered jeremy that he was going to climb the cliffs
   i told him to stay away from the cliffs she said as they are crumbling and dangerous
   perhaps i misheard jeremy suggested im sorry
   mrs cannon was not in doubt
   when he comes back she said angrily he will be the one whos sorry

Work and play

   The swallow of summer, she toils all summer,
   A blue-dark knot of glittering voltage,
   A whiplash swimmer, a fish of the air.
      But the serpent of cars that crawls through the dust
      In shimmering exhaust
      Searching to slake
      Its fever in ocean
      Will play and be idle or else it will bust.

The swallow of summer, the barbed harpoon,
She flings from the furnace, a rainbow of purples,
Dips her glow in the pond and is perfect.
      But the serpent of cars that collapsed at the beach
      Disgorges its organs
      A scamper of colours
      Which roll like tomatoes
      Nude as tomatoes
      With sand in their creases
      To cringe in the sparkle of rollers and screech.

The swallow of summer, the seamstress of summer,
She scissors the blue into shapes and she sews it,
She draws a long thread and she knots it at corners.
   But the holiday people
   Are laid out like wounded
   Flat as in ovens
   Roasting and basting
   With faces of torment as space burns them blue
   Their heads are transistors
   Their teeth grit on sand grains
   Their lost kids are squalling
   While man-eating flies
   Jab electric shock needles but what can they do?

They can climb in their cars with raw bodies, raw faces
   And start up the serpent
   And headache it homeward
   A car full of squabbles
   And sobbing and stickiness
   With sand in their crannies
   Inhaling petroleum
   That pours from the foxgloves
   While the evening swallow
The swallow of summer, cartwheeling through crimson,
Touches the honey-slow river and turning
Returns to the hand stretched from under the eaves –
A boomerang of rejoicing shadow.

                                      TED HUGHES

Talking about the poem

1 Why is this poem called *Work and Play*?
2 How are the lives of the swallow and holidaymakers contrasted?
3 How is the flight of the swallow described?
4 What happens to the holidaymakers during their time at the seaside?
5 Comment on the effectiveness of the comparisons Ted Hughes uses.
6 What views of summer does the poet seem to hold?
7 Do you agree with him?

Writing your own poem

The drawing on page 143 shows a boat on a beach. It is rather different to the beach where the holidaymakers 'roast and baste' in Ted Hughes's poem.

A beach like the one in the picture can provide many interesting discoveries. Who owns the boat? Is it still used, or is it derelict? What is in the rock pools? Are there caves nearby? What has the tide brought in?

Write a poem called 'On the sand'.

Vocabulary

Each of the following prefixes can turn words into their opposites:
dis- (as in *dis*appear)
in- (as in *in*accurate)
non- (as in *non*sense)
un- (as in *un*fortunate)

Give five more examples of words using each of these prefixes (twenty examples in all), then use each example in a sentence.

Further reading

Jill Paton Walsh's books include:

Goldengrove
Goldengrove is Grandmother's seaside home in Cornwall. There Madge meets Paul, whom she believes to be her cousin. They spend their summers exploring the Cornish seashore, but one summer a disturbing stranger arrives.

The Dolphin Crossing
During World War Two John's family home in a village is used as a hospital. John and a new friend, Pat, an unwilling evacuee from London, feel they can make little contribution to the war effort until they set out in the 'Dolphin' to help in the evacuation at Dunkirk.

Fireweed
A realistic story of a pair of runaways hiding from the authorities during the terrifying Blitz in London, during 1940.

After attending a convent school Barbara Willard tried acting. She later turned to writing and worked in the story department of several major film companies. Her books include:

The Battle of Wednesday Week
Nicholas and Charlotte did not really like the idea of sharing their holiday cottage with four young Americans. Far away in New England, Nan, Lucy, Alan and Roderick were feeling every bit as disturbed and disgruntled.

Harrow and Harvest
Family loyalties are threatened and divisions appear as sides are taken during the Civil War.

The Grove of Green Holly
Rafe's burning ambition is to become an actor but the Puritans have closed all the playhouses. With his grandfather, old Gregory Trundle, who was once in Shakespeare's company, he establishes a refuge for out-of-work actors until the King returns and the players will once more return to favour.

Barbara Willard has also written several historical novels based on the Ashdown Forest in Sussex. These are called the Mantlemass novels. Some are listed below:

A Cold Wind Blowing
'I fear her. What she may be – or what she may do. I never spoke with any like her!' Piers Medley so describes the mysterious girl, placed in his care by a dying man.

The Lark and the Laurel
Cecily Jolland, cosseted by her father, finds it hard to come to terms with her new life in the Sussex countryside.

The Iron Lily
When her mother dies, Lilias learns she does not belong in the household that reared her. She departs to marry a rough iron worker and eventually becomes an iron master in her own right.